To Saint Abby,
May you always Know the
freedom that is Jesus
Christ. It was for freedom
that Christ set you free.

Your Servant,
Greg Skipper.

Thou Givest . . . They Gather

Thou Givest...
They Gather

AMY CARMICHAEL

"That Thou givest them they gather:

Thou openest Thine hand, they are filled with good."

Psalm 104:28

CHRISTIAN LITERATURE CRUSADE
Fort Washington, Pennsylvania 19034

CHRISTIAN LITERATURE CRUSADE
U.S.A.
Box 1449, Fort Washington, PA 19034
CANADA
Box 189, Elgin, Ontario KOG 1EO

©1958 Dohnavur Fellowship
This American edition 1971 under
special arrangement with
Dohnavur Fellowship
This printing 1988
ISBN 0-87508-083-9

PRINTED IN THE UNITED STATES OF AMERICA

CONTENTS

INTRODUCTION

IN THE extreme south of India, near the village of Dohnavur, God has brought into being a work which centres around Indian children saved from an upbringing leading to an evil life.

Miss Amy Carmichael, a British missionary who arrived in India in 1895 and continued there until her death in 1951, was one of the first on whom God laid the burden of these children's need. Through her response in obedience and faith, the foundations were laid of what later became the Dohnavur Fellowship, as in the course of the years she and her Indian helpers were joined by a number of men and women from overseas.

Beginning with two or three children, there are now many hundreds in the "Family". Some have already grown up and become fellow-workers, caring for the children, tending the sick in Hospital (which is open to the people of the countryside), or sharing in various other activities of the Fellowship. There is a small holiday home in the forested mountain country, about 3000 feet up, with its river and pool which are sometimes referred to in these pages. This is a few miles west of Dohnavur, which itself is set in the plains.

Miss Carmichael was known to Indian and European alike as *Amma,* which is the Tamil word for mother. By this name she also became known, through her books and

1

through her letters, to friends all over the world who by their prayers and gifts set forward the work. An accident in 1931, followed by illness, confined her almost entirely to her room for the remaining years of her life. Although often in pain she wrote much during that time, and also for the greater part of it continued as leader of the Fellowship and Family.

One of the ways in which she kept in touch with her Family was by sharing through written or dictated Notes some spiritual lesson which she herself was learning or had learnt afresh. Taught and led of God through difficulties and disappointments, she was able to tell, from her own experience, of His faithfulness and of the absolute reliability of His promises for all who put their trust in Him and take the Bible as their rule of life.

It is these Notes which are referred to in the Foreword which follows. It has been written by Miss Mary Mills, who came to Dohnavur in 1920. She nursed Amma after the accident and was her constant companion during the years of illness. Many of the Notes were originally shared with her, and with the help of Miss Beatrice Taylor she has prepared this and an earlier collection of them for publication.

1958   J. E. RISK

FOREWORD

WHEN WE were going through Amma's notes, from which we eventually compiled the little book of Daily Readings, *Edges of His Ways,* we found that there were many that we longed to include, but which had to be left behind for a time. These we now bring to you, believing that you will be glad to have them, and believing, too, that the Lord gave and she gathered, that others might share the harvest.

They covered many years and the needs known to her during them, with their varied circumstances and occasions; and because they helped and comforted many, we feel led to pass them on.

She was always ready to gather what He is always ready to give, and to her there were no experiences in life to which the Bible did not open out the Way, the Truth, and the Life — no problems which are not met by the promises found therein.

There was never any idea of publication when she shared these thoughts with her Family; and we have not used them in any chronological order, but have arranged them in sections according to subjects. They do not cover nearly all the ground into which her thinking led her along these particular lines, yet we believe that those who read may be led further by the Lord Himself into depths of which they surely give more than a glimpse; and as we send them out we pray that indeed some may find, as she did, the truth of those words, *Thou openest Thine hand, they are filled with good.*

To this I add a few words written by her to her Family with reference to those messages. I think she would like you to have them:

> I do thank you, so many of you, who have let me know that these notes have carried messages from His heart to yours. Sometimes what appears to be given to me for you, does not seem to fit the need of all — at least, I always think of some whose need it may *not* fit. And yet, often it has been those very words that have carried something from Him. So I leave it, in tranquillity, and write what comes, believing that in this way (the only way by which I can reach out to you) He will not leave me without guidance.

We should not like to leave unmentioned our gratitude to those of the Fellowship who have lovingly contributed their help during the preparation of this book, for indeed it owes much to their unstinted giving in every kind of way.

Dohnavur, Tirunelveli Dist., S. India.   M.M.

Note about Abbreviations

A.V.	— Authorized Version
R.V.	— Revised Version of 1881
Am. R.V.	— American Committee's 1901 Edition of the R.V.
P.B.V.	— Prayer Book Version
Con.	— Conybeare
Del.	— Delitzsch
Moff.	— Moffatt
Roth.	— Rotherham
Weym.	— Weymouth
LXX	— The Septuagint

Quotations

Care has been taken in verifying quotations from the different versions; but in some cases, where the setting calls for special emphasis, italics and capitals which are not found in the version concerned have been used in this book.

Capitals have also been used for personal pronouns and some titles relating to the Deity, in accordance with common practice, although this does not always conform to the versions as published.

In some versions (e.g. Weymouth) renderings differ in different editions; in others (e.g. Rotherham) there are special marks of emphasis and punctuation which cannot be reproduced in a book like this.

Verses of poetry not in quotation marks are from Amma's own writings unless otherwise stated.

CHAPTER 1

"THY TESTIMONIES ARE MY DEAR DELIGHT"

Psalm 119.24, Roth.

THE amazing thing is that everyone who reads the Bible has the same joyful thing to say about it. In every land, in every language, it is the same tale: where that Book is read, not with the eyes only, but with the mind and heart, the life is changed. Sorrowful people are comforted, sinful people are transformed, people who were in the dark walk in the light. Is it not wonderful to think that this Book, which is such a mighty power if it gets a chance to work in an honest heart, is in our hands today? And we can read it freely, no man making us afraid.

Isa. 8.11, Roth.: *Thus spake Jehovah unto me like a firm grasp of the hand.* . . .

Blessed be the Lord our God who does in very truth cause His word to come unto us in this way.

Sometimes this firm grasp comes through the opening of a single word. It has come to me through such an opening of the word "trust", which I find in Young* means to *lean on — trust — confide.* I found that Rotherham sometimes translates it *lean on* as in 2 Chronicles 14.11, "On Thee do

*Young's *Analytical Concordance to the Bible.*

7

we lean"; and chapter 16.7, "Because thou . . . hast not
leaned"; and I found many verses in the Psalms in which
are very comfortable words so translated.

Psa. 13.5: "I have trusted in Thy mercy" — *leaned on*
Thy mercy, "Thy loving-kindness", as others render it; that
loving-kindness which has loved us with an everlasting love,
which pardons and cleanses and will never tire of us. Lord,
I lean upon Thy loving-kindness. And Psa. 32.10: "He
that trusteth in the Lord [leaneth on the Lord], mercy
[loving-kindness] shall compass him about."

Is it not like His love to let us know that He wants us
to lean, not only on His loving-kindness, but on His very
self? "Now there was leaning on Jesus' bosom one of His
disciples, whom Jesus loved",[1] the word takes us there;
Whoso *leaneth* on the Lord, happy is he.[2] He is indeed.

That same verb is used in some of the verses that are
never far from us, such as Psalm 143.8, Cause me to hear
. . . for on Thee do I *lean*. (It was when John was leaning, that he heard his Lord's answer to a question which
puzzled the others.)

What time I am afraid, I will *lean* on Thee. Psa. 56.3.

I will *lean,* and not be afraid. Isa. 12.2.

Thou wilt keep him in perfect peace . . . because he
leaneth on Thee; . . . *Lean ye* on the Lord for ever: for
in the Lord Jehovah is everlasting strength. Isa. 26.3, 4.

Can we wonder that the blessed Spirit who guides in the
choice of words, led the writer who was longing to tell of
the delight of answered prayer, to this special verb, which
so clearly shows that it is nothing in us which accounts for
the Lord's goodness to us? It is all, all of Him. The Lord
is my strength and my shield; my heart *leaned* on Him, and
I am helped: therefore my heart greatly rejoiceth; and with
my song will I praise Him. Psa. 28.7.

May the Lord of love make this word of His to be "like a firm grasp of the hand" to each one of us.

      [1]Jn. 13.23.   [2]Prov. 16.20.

Gen. 18.33: *And the Lord went His way, as soon as He had left communing with Abraham.*

As soon as He had left — as if to remind us that the great thing in such times with Him is what *He* says, not what *we* say. It is interesting that the Hebrew word used here is *darbar* — our "durbar";* and at a durbar what matters most is what the king, or whoever is greatest there, says and does. So in our times alone with our Lord we should not forget to listen. The Bible is full of stories of unrestrained, long, loving prayer; but it tells us enough of what a "durbar" is to make us understand that He, to whom we speak, can so speak to us that we shall recognize not only the Voice, but the words that the Voice is saying.

Do any, to whom these matters are new, wonder what I mean? I mean something quite simple and yet very wonderful. When reading your Bible have you not often noticed that some word has shone out and seemed to speak in a new, direct, clear way to you? It has been as though you had never read it before. You cannot explain the vivid freshness, the *life,* in it, the extraordinary way it has leapt to your eye — to your heart. It just *was* so. That was the "durbar"; you were in the very presence of your King at that moment. He was speaking to you. His word was spirit and life. "The words that I speak unto you, they are spirit, and they are life."[1]

Durbar — A public audience or levee held by a native prince, or by a British sovereign, governor or viceroy, in India.

"Durbar", as we use the word in India, usually means a grand occasion, like the Delhi Durbar. But "durbar" originally meant just *word,* and to *speak.* It is used of the simple talking together of friend with friend, David with Abigail, for example, and many others. It does not necessarily imply a great event.

An illustration of how simple a durbar may be came in this way: I was on the verandah and saw someone passing. The next moment he was beside me, though I had not seen him come. That is the way our dear Lord does:

> "How entered, by what secret stair
> I know not, knowing only He was there."*

Then for a minute we spoke together (that was our earthly durbar), and then we spoke to our King together (that was our Heavenly durbar); and the next moment he was off about his Father's business. That tiny durbar had sweetened the hour.

Perhaps some may wonder, "How shall I know when He is speaking to me? How can I distinguish between the voices I hear in my heart? I am not old or wise or clever, how can I know?" How does a baby know the voice of the one it loves best? Is it old, or wise, or clever? A sheep is not a clever animal, but it knows the voice of its shepherd, and a stranger will it not follow, for it knows not the voice of strangers.[2] *Love* is the answer to all our questions; love, and we shall know.

[1]Jn. 6.63.   [2]Jn. 10.4, 5.

*T. E. Brown.

Gen. 32.31: *And as he passed over Penuel the sun rose upon him.*

More than fifty years ago a man who had met his Lord in the sunrise stood by the long breakfast-table in the *China Inland Mission* House, Shanghai, and said these words: "*This* is the day which the Lord hath made; we will rejoice and be glad in it."[1] I was one who sat at that table, and those words fell into my heart like seeds of light. Many a time since then, especially when it was dull weather in my soul, these words have enlightened me and help has come. How much I should have missed, if it had not been that the sun rose upon that man before he came down to breakfast that morning.

May the Lord give it to us so to meet Him before we meet others. I was reading the other day of one who was always "in low gear" in the morning. Halting or not, "low gear" is not for us. "The voice of joy and health"[2] is in the dwelling of him who stands in the sunrise with his God, and wherever he goes, he will sow seeds of light.

[1]Psa. 118.24.   [2]Psa. 118.15, P.B.V.

Mark 6.56: *As many as touched Him were made whole.*

Many of you will be having your Quiet Time as I write. May each one touch at least the border of His garment. One knows when one has done that. It is different from just reading or even just praying. Something happens when we touch. What happens? Who can tell? Only we know that something has passed from Him to us — courage to do the difficult thing we had feared to do; patience to bear with that trying one; fortitude to carry on when we felt we could not; sweetness, inward happiness, peace.

God's way is to take some word in His Book and make it spirit and life. Then, relying upon that word, it is possible for us to go on from strength to strength. There is always something new in our lives which calls for vital faith, if we are to go on with God; but there is always the word waiting in His Book which will meet us just where we are and carry us further on. It will be a fight to the end — "the good fight of faith" is His word about it — but full provision is made for victory in that fight, and whether the matter that engages us has to do with our inner life or the outer, there is nothing to fear. It is our Father's good pleasure to give us the Kingdom.[1] We need never — by His grace we *shall* never — be defeated.

This note is for any who have given themselves to the service of love, yet fear lest things may become too difficult by and by, and in whose hearts the question arises, "What if I fail?" There is no need to fail. The love of God is the same yesterday and today and for ever, and one of the loving ways of love is to prepare us beforehand for what is coming later on, so that when it comes we shall not fail.

That was what happened in Rome long ago. In the year A.D. 58 (or thereabouts) a letter was read aloud in the little church at Rome. Even young children, I think, must have listened with some understanding to the great paragraph beginning "Who shall separate us from the love of Christ?"[2] As for the grown-up people — though there was no sign of persecution then — it must have become their meat and drink. And, nourished thus, they became strong, so that when in A.D. 64 the fires of Nero were lighted, they endured. The Spirit, the Comforter, who caused those words to be written in that letter six years before they were urgently required, is the same Spirit still; foreseeing all. He prepares us for all. Perhaps today some word will reach us that is meant to prepare us for our tomorrow. Let us not miss that word.

[1]Luke 12.32.   [2]Rom. 8.35-39.

Many times lately my Bible has opened at Psalm 119, and verse 11 has caught my eye: "Thy word have I hid in mine heart, that I might not sin against Thee." That verse is really the fragment of the story of a brave life. The date of the Psalm is not certain, but it is clear that it was written in very difficult times, and here the writer tells how it was that he stood firm. He had the storehouse of his mind full of treasure (different translations bring out the thought of storing treasure). His heart was full of the words of his God; they were there, ready to help him, however hard things were.

Sometimes in the night when I could not sleep, comfort and help that I never can tell have come through the beautiful words of our Book flowing over my mind like cool waters.

Here are three ways of putting treasure into our storehouse:

1. Whenever the Spirit of God makes a word live to you, take time to let that word sink deep into your heart. This way is open to us all.

2. Whenever the Bible is read aloud listen with the inward ear. Then, whether you can immediately recall it or not, it is stored in that wonderful storehouse of memory, and in time of need it will be there for use. This, too, is a way open to us all.

3. This way is, perhaps, only open to the fairly young. If we do not use it when we can, we lose more than can be told. It is the way we call learning by heart.

I suggest that you choose chapters like Isaiah 53, John 14, 15, 16, 17, or Psalms like 27, 91 and others, or paragraphs like Romans 8.31-39, and learn them steadily verse by verse. Keep a dated record, and you will be astonished to find how much you have put in your storehouse by the end of a year.

Psa. 114.7, 8, P.B.V.: *The God of Jacob who turned the hard rock into a standing water, and the flint-stone into a springing well [a fountain of waters. A.V.]*

There was a time when I had to prepare a dear child for a great trial. I knew, though she did not, all that was involved, and everything in me was bent on preparing her to stand strong. Every verse I taught her, every chorus I wrote for her, was bent that way. I learned then more of the heart of God than I had ever known before. Through the love — watchful, constant, set on strengthening and enabling — that He had given to me, He taught me something of the ways of His love.

St. Paul speaks of things said by permission, not of commandment.[1] Speaking so, I would suggest that it is the custom of our Father to do for us just what I tried to do for that beloved child. I believe that, knowing what we shall be called to face, today, tomorrow, He so plans that in our reading beforehand, there will be exactly the word that will carry us through. That new experience is meant to give us a glorious opportunity to test and prove the word which He has given us.

Sometimes the special word may be given through another child of God, sometimes through some other part of the Book than the place of our usual reading. But God seems to love the ordinary, and it is in the ordinary we mostly find Him. Whichever way He comes to us in preparation, the one thing that matters is that we should be sensitive to His touch, even though, like the child I taught, we do not in the least know what He is doing.

Looking back over these many years, I see the hard rock and the flint-stone turned to standing water, clear pools, springing wells, fountains of water.

Shall we look out more carefully for these words that are meant to fortify and rejoice our hearts? Nothing can make up for them, and nothing can draw us closer to our Father than these intimate, tender touches of His love.

[1] Cor. 7.6.

Psa. 119.77, P.B.V.: *O let Thy loving mercies come unto me, that I may live: for Thy law is my delight.*

We all know what it is to feel withered (at least most of us probably do) and then suddenly to be revived. The loving mercies of the Lord, flowing like a river, have come unto us and we live, we sing. "My heart danceth for joy, and in my song will I praise Him",[1] "for Thy law is my delight."

These glorious, strong, vivid words are most refreshing and exhilarating. Yesterday there was a word in one of the Psalms which the loving mercy of the Lord did truly turn to delight for me: "Thou hast loosed my bonds" — "broken my bonds in sunder."[2] What bonds He has broken in the story of this work — *bonds broken in sunder* might be the name of a whole book. And in our own hearts' stories, too, we know of many a bond no human hand could have loosened, but He has broken it in sunder.

To what end? Another of the Psalms for that day answers the question — that we may be bound by other bonds: "Bind the sacrifice with cords, yea, even unto the horns of the altar."[3] "Thy testimonies have I claimed as mine heritage for ever: and why? they are the very joy of my heart."[4]

Scattered through the Bible we have words like these that carry us straight through the seen into the unseen. And they are all gathered up in 2 Corinthians 4.16-18. Gaze deep into those three verses, and you are where St. John was when he wrote, "After this I looked, and behold, a door was opened in Heaven."[5] I want to live looking through that door, living as one who truly believes that the temporal matters not at all; only the Eternal is important.

[1]Psa. 28.8, P.B.V   [2]Psa. 116.16 [14, P.B.V.]
[3]Psa. 118.27, P.B.V.   [4]Psa. 119.111, P.B.V.   [5]Rev. 4.1.

I have come more and more to watch for those minute touches of the love and forethought of our Father which are shown in the smallest things of life, such as the coming of a flower, a message, a picture, a letter, a book; the touch of a loving hand, the look in loving eyes, the tones in loving voices — things too small to tell, but making such a difference to our day. In the same way, in our Bibles and in *Daily Light*,* let us watch for the "chance" word, the repeated word of assurance and strength. Here is one which has meant much to me. I would not write it now if it were not that I know there are some who will find something very good in it. On March 3, 1893, the day I sailed for Japan, and on November 30, 1896, the day I left Bangalore

*Bagster's *Daily Light on the Daily Path* — a small book of Scripture verses grouped together in topics for morning and evening meditation throughout the year.

for what I afterwards knew was the appointed service, for which the three preceding years were preparation, the word in *Daily Light* was the same: "And he said unto Him, If Thy presence go not with me, carry us not up hence. For wherein shall it be known here that I and Thy people have found grace in Thy sight? is it not in that Thou goest with us?"[1]   But that Presence does go with us — "My presence shall go with thee"[2] — wherever He shall send us; not only then, but through this day, wherever it be spent, however it be spent — "for Thou art with me; Thy rod and Thy staff, they comfort me."   And the day will come when He will carry us up hence, and we "shall dwell in the house of the Lord for ever."

[1]Exod. 33.15, 16.   [2]*v*. 14.

CHAPTER 2

"MY GOD WITH HIS LOVING-KINDNESS WILL MEET ME"

Psalm 59.10, Am. R.V.

JULIAN of Norwich wrote, "It is God's will that we take His comfortings as largely and as mightly as we may take them, and also He willeth that we take our troubles as lightly as we may take them, and set them at nought."

Yes, for "joy cometh in the morning."[1]

> Lord, I would take Thy comfortings
>   With both hands gratefully,
> And griefs' dark overshadowings
>   As lightly as may be.
> For they belong to evenings,
>   Joy comes with day to me,
> Comes running with the day to me.
>
> Although my wayside inn at night
>   May harbour Grief as guest,
> With dawn he swiftly takes his flight;
>   And like a bird to nest,
> Dear Joy comes singing with delight,
>   As she comes home to rest;
> Dear Joy comes singing[2] home to rest.

[1]Psa. 30.5.　　[2]See mar.

"I cannot get the way of Christ's love. Had I known what He was keeping for me, I should never have been so faint-hearted", Samuel Rutherford wrote long ago. Have we not often had cause to say so too? But if for a season we are in heaviness, if the morning after a night of pain, or prayer, or fierce fight of temptation, or any other weariness, finds us arid as a burnt-up bit of land, there is a perfect word waiting to hearten us: *Grace to help in time of need* — in time of need — that is the word. Often and often I have drunk of that living water very thirstily. Blessed be God for this brook in the way. "For we have not a high priest that cannot be touched with the feeling of our infirmities; but One that hath been in all points tempted like as we are, yet without sin. Let us therefore draw near with boldness unto the throne of grace, that we may receive mercy, and may find grace to help us in time of need." Heb. 4.15, 16, R.V.

I think you will appreciate the following words, as I did. They were sent to me by a friend in South Africa:

> "He has for thee
> A light for every shadow,
> A plan for each tomorrow,
> A key for every problem,
> A balm for every sorrow."

God never leaves us with only one line of comfort, there are many always at hand. There is one that I have not often heard mentioned, and yet there is help to be found in it. "Thou shalt not be given into the hand of the men of whom thou art afraid."[1] What is the thing that you most fear and

most earnestly pray about, the thing of all other things that
you dread? If you love your Lord, and yet know your own
weakness, is it not that something may happen to sweep
you off your feet, or that your strength may be drained and
you may yield and fall, and fail Him at the end? I have
known many whose lives were shadowed by this fear.

Oh, take comfort. The God who knew the heart of His
servant Ebed-melech knows our hearts, too. He knows
who the men are (what the forces of trial are) of whom we
are afraid; and He assures us and reassures us, "Thou shalt
not be given into the hand of the men of whom thou art
afraid."

[1]Jer. 39.17.

Psa. 94.19, LXX: *Thy consolations have soothed my soul.*

A footnote says, "Literally, *have loved,* and the Alexan-
drine version, *have gladdened.*" Our Authorized Version
has *delight* (in the present tense), and the Prayer Book
Version, *refreshed.* Love soothes, Love gladdens, Love
delights, Love refreshes.

A few minutes before I read this I had read in Richard
Rolle (who has been for nearly 700 years in the joy of his
Lord), "Nothing is merrier than Jesu to sing, nothing more
delightful than Jesu to hear. Hearing, it truly mirths the
mind; and song uplifts it." The happy words are in tune
with what I meant to give you; for this morning in the
golden dawn after the rain, the forest was full of the singing
of birds, the very leaves of the trees seemed to sing.*

There are times when in the multitude of our thoughts
within us ("anxious thoughts", is Darby's translation),

*This note was written from the Forest.

nothing in all the world can do anything for us but the consolations of our God. These times can come even in the happy days of preparation for service, and in the service too. But the comforts of God come close to us. They love us, and loving us they soothe, gladden, delight, refresh. "Nothing is merrier than Jesu to sing. . . . It truly mirths the mind."

Psa. 138.8, P.B.V.: *The Lord shall make good His loving-kindness toward me.*

Every verse of Psalm 138 is pure gold, but the last verse feeds me today. With it came these words from Psalm 57.2 (also Prayer Book Version), "I will call unto the most high God, even unto the God that shall perform the cause which I have in hand."

What is the cause which I have in hand? Each one of us has a "cause" and most of us have several — inward matters of the spirit, outward matters that touch the work committed to us.

Even so, "the Lord shall make good His loving-kindness toward me", and He "shall perform the cause which I have in hand."

Isa. 64.5: *Thou meetest him that rejoiceth and worketh righteousness, those that remember Thee in Thy ways.*

What a glorious brook by the way! and to make its water sweeter, add this from Psalm 50.23, "Whoso offereth the sacrifice of thanksgiving glorifieth Me; and prepareth a way that I may show him the salvation of God",[1] and Romans

15.13: "The God of hope fill you with all joy and peace in believing, that ye may abound in hope, through the power of the Holy Ghost."

We know the great part that hope is meant to play in life by the unwearied persistence of the attack upon it. Sometimes by a long slow siege, sometimes by a sharp assault, but almost continually by something outward or inward, the great enemy of souls tries to undermine or overturn our hope; and when hope goes, joy and peace go with it. In this way he scores a triple victory and we are indeed laid low. But never, never, need it be so, for "with him is an arm of flesh; but with us is the Lord our God to help us, and to fight our battles."[2]   And our God is the God of Hope.

[1]R.V. mar.   [2]2 Chron. 32.8.

Gen. 37.17: *Let us go to Dothan.*
2 Kings 6.13: *Behold, he is in Dothan.*

The name Dothan means *Double feast.* I do not know any word in the Bible that has so often brought a double feast to me.

Elisha's Dothan takes us to Psalm 34.7: "The angel of the Lord encampeth round about them that fear Him, and delivereth them."

Joseph's Dothan takes us to Luke 7.23: "And blessed is he, whosoever shall not be offended in Me."

Which is the better? Neither. Both are God's best. In each life which follows hard after Him there will be, sooner or later, these two Dothans. Sometimes there will be glorious interventions; our God will be to us a God of deliverances upon the mountains round about. Sometimes we shall see only bare blue sky, empty hillsides, *nothing.* Then is the time to look through to the Eternal and endure "as seeing Him who is invisible."[1]

"Let us go to Dothan." Which Dothan, Lord? *He shall choose our inheritance for us, the excellency of Jacob whom He loved.*[2]

[1]Heb. 11.27.   [2]Psa. 47.4.

Certainties

I have been resting my heart on the *Certainties* this morning. They are like the mountains that abide constant, whether shining in colour, or dark in mist and rain.

In Romans 8.28 I find a *Certainty* which the great adversary continually assaults. He seems to know that if only he can smother this mountain peak in clouds, our spiritual life will be smothered too. It was so with Joseph. First at Dothan, then in Egypt, all things seemed to be working together for harm, not for good; and the human seemed to triumph over the Divine. We read of no special revelations granted for his sustenance in prison. He seems to have been trusted to walk by faith not by sight (as for the most part we are), and he had not his own finished story to read, nor Romans 8.28, nor any other Scripture. Try to imagine life without a time of blessed quiet every morning with our Bibles — and I marvel at the wonder of the grace of God as shown forth in Joseph and in countless others. For Joseph met his moments of crisis as only one who habitually walks with God can ever do. His soul entered willingly into the iron[1] of those strange, cruel, unexplained circumstances, and passing through, was purified from the least taint of earthliness. Hereafter we see him only as

receiving and reflecting the blessed love of God, and he
could say, "As for you, ye thought evil against me; but God
meant it unto good."[2]

Thank God for this *Certainty*. The effect of man's sin
or mistake; disappointment over souls; temptations to discouragement about ourselves or anything else; all limitations
and frustrations, and all trials of the flesh and spirit, are
working together (with all the thousand joys that are our
Father's servants too) for good, His golden good, to us who
love God.

[1]Psa. 105.18, R.V. mar.   [2]Gen. 50.20.

Gen. 40.7: *Wherefore look ye so sadly today?*

If we are spending our sympathy upon ourselves, we
have none to spare for others. Joseph had good reason to
pity himself, to sympathize with himself, and to ask others
to be sorry for him and sympathize with him. But we find
nothing of that here.

> "I ask Thee for a thoughtful love
>   Through constant watchings wise . . .
> And a heart at leisure from itself
>   To soothe and sympathize."*

The life of Joseph from this time on is that prayer turned
into deeds.

There are two verses in the Old Testament which come
to me when I think of this: "The Spirit of the Lord shall
rest upon Him, . . . and shall make Him of quick understanding in the fear of the Lord".[1] "The Lord God hath

*A. L. Waring.

given me the tongue of them that are taught, that I should know how to sustain with words him that is weary"[2] — "how to succour the fainting".[3]

Joseph did not speak smooth, false words. The ear that is wakened to hear, hears truth. The tongue can only speak what the ear heard. But it was the word of truest love, for if the baker heard it aright, it prepared him to meet God. Joseph could tell him how to do that. Perhaps we shall see that baker with Joseph one day.

But the chief thought with me is this: Joseph in prison had "a heart at leisure from itself". He could listen to the voice of God morning by morning, and, I am sure, often through the day; he could hear, and be quick of understanding in the fear of the Lord, quick to notice another's needs, strong to sustain with words, and loving enough to succour. So may it be with us. So shall we be able to lead others out of the waste lands of dullness and heaviness, and perhaps bitterness, into "the light of the knowledge of the glory of God".[4]

Lord, give it to us to live this life.

> *Not I, but Christ:*
> *Not self, but others.*

[1] Isa. 11.2, 3.   [2] Isa. 50.4, R.V.   [3] Roth.   [4] 2 Cor. 4.6.

Gen. 41.45: *Zaphnath-paaneah*

"The man to whom secrets are revealed" was the king's name for Joseph.[1] If our King were speaking of us could He give us that name? Are we in His confidence? There is a most searching and illuminating word about this: "The froward [perverse, R.V.] is abomination to the Lord: but His secret is with the righteous [the upright, R.V.]."[2] God

can show us nothing of the deeper things of His word and
His ways if we are at all perverted from His purpose, self-
willed in any detail. Are we? I have found that the *I* has
a most persistent way of wanting things not given, or wanting to do something, or be somewhere, apart from His
evident appointment. To yield to that wish of the *I* is to
be perverse, perverted from the intention of our God,
crooked. To refuse it is to be straight.

Suppose we suddenly realize that we are wanting our own
will, and so, in His sight, are perverted, crooked; what are
we to do? Go to the story in Luke 13.11-13. That woman
had been bound for eighteen years, but eighteen seconds, or
even only eight, give time enough for Satan to bind. We
cannot lift ourselves up. But the Lord can say to us, "Thou
art loosed", and "immediately" we are made straight. And
"immediately", just as if nothing had happened, so mighty
are the powers of the precious Blood, we are back in the
confidence of our God.

Oh, what a God is ours! Not only the meaning of
dreams, which are sometimes from Him — if we live in
His Presence day and night, dreams may be "the sound of
His footsteps" — but in all common ways, through all
common days, He will open to us the meaning of things,
and especially the needs of other souls. We may all be His
Zaphnath-paaneahs.

[1]Gen. 41.45, mar.   [2]Prov. 3.32.

Heb. 12.3: *Consider Him . . . lest ye be wearied and
faint in your minds.*

"Turning our eyes away from all else toward Jesus" is
Way's rendering of the words, "looking unto Jesus", in the

previous verse. This quiet word about a long considering look follows that. Consider His life from the day when for the first time He took a hammer and a nail in His hands and learned how to use them, to the day when another used a hammer and nails, and what do we see? Look at His last recorded joy before He suffered — the coming of the Greeks — it is followed instantly by the eternal "Except" of suffering, and then, "Now is My soul troubled".[1]

There is a Hebrew word translated "faint", meaning *to show self feeble*. Proverbs 24.10 can make one ashamed: If thou *show thyself feeble* in the day of adversity, thy strength is small; but there is another Hebrew word with the same meaning, and it, like Hebrews 12.2, opens the way out: "When my soul fainted within me [showed itself feeble] I remembered the Lord".[2]

We have more to remember than Jonah had. He had not our Lord Jesus. After strain of any sort, and after great blessing and joy, the mind is strangely sensitive to the kind of attack that leads to fainting. Sometimes after the glow of victory, suddenly there is faintness. Then is the moment to consider Him who endured. I do not know of any way of escape so sure and so swift as a long steady look at our beloved Lord; and then, having escaped that snare of the fowler, let us do what the bird does — sing.

[1]Jn. 12.20-27.   [2]Jonah 2.7.

Pause

This is the word in the LXX for *Selah*. The first time it occurs is in Psalm 3.2: "Many there be which say of my soul, There is no help for him in God." *Pause*. "But Thou, O Lord, art my helper". (I use the LXX version

here because the word *helper* so perfectly balances the
"There is no help".)

We all know the weary voices that sometimes seem to fill
the very air. "There is no help". The voices can murmur
and mutter the same words about many things. "There is
no help . . ." *Pause*. "But Thou, O Lord, art my helper".
With that word comes peace and courage to go on.

It is so also in the inward temptations of life. They can
all be turned to peace if only, instead of answering, or as it
were arguing with, the voices of the enemy, we *pause,* and
then look up. "There is no help . . ." *Pause*. "But Thou,
O Lord . . ."

Many scholars believe, however, that the *Selah* signifies a
sudden pealing forth of musical instruments. The *Pause,*
they think, was for praise. Let us then fill our pauses with
praise, giving all that in us lies to pure praise, pure adoration, the loving worship of the grateful heart.

Psa. 60.4: *Thou hast given a banner to them that fear
Thee, that it may be displayed because of the truth.*

After this glorious word about the banner, there is a
Selah. If the word there was the sign for a sounding of
trumpets, a shout of triumph, then the thought is praise
before we see the victory; but I think it may possibly have
been the other kind of *Selah,* the sign for a Pause, even in
the thick of the fight. This at least is the kind we must
often have, if we are to go on to do valiantly; and sometimes I wonder if there is anything else the devil contests
with greater determination. The moment we set ourselves
to be quiet and seek our God in stillness, there is a clamour
about us; we remember things we should do, or have for-

gotten to do; we are disturbed in a hundred ways — anything to break into that *Selah*. All this is simply proof of how much it matters that we should have it. It would not be so contested if it did not matter. There is a kind of comfort in this.

So let us take heart and not give way, and not be discouraged, even though, like the old Puritan, we are "some time in getting access." We have a God who understands.

Luke 8.25: *He commandeth even the winds and water, and they obey Him.*

Even. Is there anything you find quite impossible to command in your circumstances or character? something as deaf to comand as the winds and the water? something that has baffled you a thousand times, and appears as if it would win in the end? Do not despair. "Better hath He been for years than thy fears". Better can He be, far better. He can command even this that seems as if it would not be commanded. Let that "even" be a comfort to you. "He commandeth even the winds and water, and they obey Him." He can say to that "even" of yours, "Peace, be still"; and there will be "a great calm." Mark 4.39.

Is there one who is facing something that seems impossible? Does the appointed burden feel too heavy to be carried? the disappointment too sharp to be welcomed? the duty too toilsome to be performed with joy? "You have not to do it in your unaided strength: it is God who is all the while supplying the impulse, giving you the power to resolve, the strength to perform, the execution of His goodpleasure."[1] And so, "I am equal to every lot, through the help of Him who gives me inward strength."[2]

And here is another beautiful word written down long, long ago for us: "Thy God hath sent forth strength for thee";[3] so we need never be weak. We can be sure that every day strength is sent forth for us. So we need never be defeated, but can always be strong in the strength of our mighty God.

All the tremendous forces of Nature in the world today are at the call of our God, and are only a faint shadow of the spiritual power that is His, and that He is ready to put forth for us. Is it not amazing? How utterly foolish it is to plead weakness when we, even we, may (if we will) move into the stream of that power.

[1]Phil. 2.13, Way.   [2]Phil. 4.13, Way.   [3]Psa. 68.28, P.B.V.

Psa. 59.10, Am. R.V.: *My God with His loving-kindness will meet me.*

To some of us sometimes there comes such a sense of the vastness of things and of our own insignificance, that it can all but shake our faith in the truth that our Father regards the fall of a sparrow. To me, one of the proofs of the Divine in this marvelous Book is the way, continually, and as it were unconsciously, it meets just this in us, and answers it, not always by a statement, but often by a story, a simple loving little story of something that truly happened.

Daniel, overwhelmed by the vision of the majestic march of history and the glory of the Lord, "retained no strength", "and behold, an hand touched me."[1] John, looking through the very thin veil of time into Eternity, and seeing his Lord (the Lord he had seen pierced) in whose hand were seven stars, suddenly falls into uttermost weakness, "I fell at His feet as dead." And then, just as though there were no seven stars, "He laid His right hand upon me."[2]   Is it not beautiful that there is no rebuke, and that there never is, for the weakness of the human?   "And the soul of the wounded calleth for help, and God doth not regard it as foolish."[3] He comforts, He lays His right hand on the soul wounded by weariness, or fear, or any kind of weakness, and He says, as though that one were the only one in all the universe, "O man greatly beloved, fear not: peace be unto thee, be strong, yea, be strong."[4]   And when He has thus spoken unto us, we are strengthened.

> O Thou in whose right hand were seven stars,
> And whose right hand was on Thy servant laid,
> How tender was Thy touch, Thy word, Be not afraid.
> Thou who didst say, O man greatly beloved,
> Fear not, and, Peace be unto thee, be strong,
> What wealth of grace and mercy doth to Thee belong.
>
> Thy touch, Thy word, and lo, like to a cloud
> That was but is not in the fields of air,
> So is the fear we feared; we look, it is not there,
> Dissolved, departed, banished by Thy touch.
> Oh, as we pray, purge us from every fear,
> Thou who dost hold the stars, our Lord,
>   art Thou not here?

[1]Dan. 10.8, 10.   [2]Rev. 1.16, 17,   [3]Job 24.12, Roth.
                         [4]Dan. 10.19.

Matt. 14.31: *And immediately Jesus stretched forth His hand, and caught him.*

I have been feeding on the comfort of this word "immediately"; it has been speaking to me, as sometimes God's words do, by its quick lovingness. How many seconds lie between a man's beginning to sink and his sinking? Any of you who have been out of your depth in water before you could swim, or, being able to swim, were somehow powerless, will know that a single second or less, sees one who is beginning to sink, under water. How swift then, was the movement of love.

And as He was, so He is. "Must we wait till the evening to be forgiven?" a child asked once. Do we not all know that feeling? It seems too good to be true that at the very moment of consciousness of sin, or even the shadow of sin, there is immediate pardon, cleansing, the light of His blessed countenance. But nothing ever can be too good to be true with such a Lord as ours.

The use of that word 'immediately" in the Gospels makes a Bible study of hours. I must leave all that, and end with this one that has been more than ever life and peace to me of late. They were troubled, those poor men in the boat. "And *immediately* He talked with them".[1] We know what He said. He has said it to us often.

How needless their trouble seems to us as we read. Do ours seem as needless to the Heavenly watchers? Do they wonder about us, as we do about those men, how there could be room for trouble in a ship that was under His command? (It was He who had constrained them to go to the other side. It is He who directs our boat now, to the Other Side.) But there is nothing of this wonder in the sweetness of the words of our Lord Jesus when He *immediately* talked with them. He understood.

We, who know how upholding dear and loving words can be when a friend who understands does not blame, but just understands even the trouble that need not be, and comforts it, can enter into this most lovely story and find honey in this honeycomb word, *Immediately.*

> *Immediately Jesus stretched forth His hand,*
> *and caught him.*
> *Immediately He talked with them.*
> *Speak, Lord; for Thy servant heareth.*[2]

[1]Mark 6.50.   [2]1 Sam. 3.9.

Psa. 72.6: *He shall come down like rain upon the mown grass: as showers that water the earth.*

Have you ever felt like mown grass, "ready to wither beneath the summer sun, unless refreshed by rain"?[1] What renewing words these are for such days. As I read them I thought of some who may be pressed and tired; and when one is tired it is possible to feel very dry. Let them refresh you as they have refreshed me. It is wonderfully refreshing to be reminded of what we know is true.

There is a further thought from this Psalm that I want to add: "And He shall live; and one shall give to Him of Sheba's gold; and He shall make intercession continually for him, all day long shall He bless him".[2] Is this not comforting to one who feels dry and needy? Let it say to you, "Today, all day long, shall He bless me. There will not be a minute of this day which will not find my Lord blessing me, even me"; for the one who trusts Him and offers to Him something He counts more precious than Sheba's gold — the love of a grateful heart — is blessed all day long; every hour of the day is blessed. And He who blesses us all day long meets us each morning with His loving-kind-

ness, goes before us from hour to hour with His mercy,[3]
waters us, and thus He refreshes His mown grass.

[1]Kay, note.   [2]v. 15, Kay.   [3]Psa. 50.1, Am. R.V., R.V. mar.

Isa. 58.11: *Thou shalt be like a watered garden, and like a
spring of water whose waters fail not.*

A garden does not water itself; it is watered.   A spring
does not fill itself; it is filled from unseen sources.

"Thus saith the Lord that made thee, . . . Fear not,
. . . for I will pour water upon him that is thirsty, and
floods upon the dry ground".[1]   The gardens which we have
made and loved we do not leave to die of thirst.   Once I
made a garden.   I cared for it as long as I could, and then
gave it to someone else.   But that one forgot to water it,
or did not give it enough water.   One day I saw it.   I can
feel again the little sharp pang that went through me as I
saw the drooping leaves and dried-up buds; and I remember
thinking, "If only she had made that little garden herself,
she would have cared more for it."   And this is just a tiny
faint picture of what is meant by such words as, "Fear not,
. . . for I will pour water upon him that is thirsty, and
floods upon the dry ground".[1]   Never, never does our great
Gardener give His gardens away (as I gave mine).   He who
made us, waters us, pours floods of water on us when we
are thirsty.   And all this means we shall never be dried up.

The springs in our big wells bubble up unhindered; it is
not hard for water to spring up through water.   But it *is*
hard for it to spring up through sand, and yet it does.   One
day, at Cape Comorin, the children found a fresh-water
spring bubbling up through the sand on the seashore; and

often we read of springs in most unlikely places, such as deserts, which are usually deep, hot, dry sand.

"In the wilderness shall waters break out, and streams in the desert"[2] is a glorious picture of future blessing, but it is a picture of present joy too. Is there a desert in any one of us? That desert is the place from which to expect water and streams. Shall we rest our hearts upon these words? for they are true. "The parched ground shall become a pool, and the thirsty land springs of water".[3]

Does it seem as though you were *not* being watered, as though the springs were *not* bubbling up? Sometimes when we feel so, we do everything but call upon the Lord. We think sadly about our dryness; perhaps we read helpful books, and even speak of it to others, hoping that they will act as watering-cans to our dryness. David did something better: "In my distress I called upon the Lord, and cried to my God: and He did hear my voice out of His temple, and my cry did enter into His ears."[4] "I called . . . and cried". "If thou knewest . . . who it is that saith to thee, Give Me to drink; thou wouldest have asked of Him, and He would have given thee living water."[5] We know whom we have believed; we need not be thirsty, we need not be dried up. "I called . . . and cried . . . and He did hear".

[1]Isa. 44.2, 3.   [2]Isa. 35.6.   [3]Isa. 35.7.   [4]2 Sam. 22.7.   [5]Jn. 4.10.

Deut. 1.31: *In the wilderness . . . thou hast seen how that the Lord thy God bare thee, as a man doth bear his son . . . until ye came into this place.*

We are not meant to stay in the wilderness, that hungry,

thirsty, dreary, "howling"[1] place, but if by any chance this
note finds someone there, let that one take courage. *"Even
there* shall Thy hand lead me, and Thy right hand shall hold
me";[2] *even there,* "like as a father pitieth his children, so
the Lord pitieth";[3] *even there,* the Lord thy God doth bear
thee, "as a man doth bear his son".

If because of sin, or faithlessness, or over-tiredness, we
have drifted into depression — which is wilderness — do
not let us stay there. Do not say, "I have prayed and
prayed, and cannot find the way out." Of course you cannot, but your Father can carry you out. The word is, "The
Lord thy God bare thee . . . in all the way that ye went,
until ye came into this place", the place where your soul
is meant to dwell, the place of "munitions of rocks", where
your bread shall be given you and your waters shall be
sure.[4]

Truly ours is a goodly heritage, O God our Father; we
are Thy little children; carry us into this place.

[1]Deut. 32.10.   [2]Psa. 139.10.   [3]Psa. 103.13.   [4]Isa. 33.16.

1 Pet. 5.10, Moff.: *The God of all grace who has called
you to His eternal glory in Christ Jesus, will repair and
recruit and strengthen you.*

Psa. 80.17, P.B.V.: *Let Thy hand be upon the Man of
Thy right hand: and upon the Son of man, whom Thou
madest so strong for Thine own self.*

Here are two verses of reassurance and joy. The Man
of God's right hand must first mean our Lord Jesus, but He
allows us to take words spoken first to Him, and use them
for ourselves; and what a word this is! *Strong for Thine
own self* — not for the sake of the joy of feeling strong and

fit, do we ask for strength, but for something far deeper. And what treasures of strong consolation are in Peter's words, which he has proved true himself, and now he shares with us all: The God of all grace, pardoning, patient, hopeful, loving, will repair and recruit and strengthen us, on to the end.

Psalm 90.14-17.

These verses make a glorious heartening prayer for each morning.   "Satisfy us in the morning with Thy mercy".[1] Satisfied in the morning — helped in the morning. (Kay refers us to Psalm 46.5, where "right early" means literally "at the facing, or turning or appearing, of morning.")   If we are helped and satisfied, then we are ready to walk through the hours of the day, not with the wobbly, shuffling, uncertain walk that a touch may upset, but with steady strength.   "In the light of Thy countenance shall they firmly march along".[2]

"Let the beauty of the Lord our God be upon us".   I think this is one of the loveliest of Bible prayers; we should never have prayed it of ourselves.   It would have felt too much to ask.   But every clause of this great prayer is wonderful.   I have been turning the tenses of the verbs to present and then to future, and I think if any of you take the time to do that, you will end, as I have, in adoration for which at first no words came.   And then — "Unto Him that loved us, and washed us from our sins in His own blood, and hath made us kings and priests unto God and His Father; to Him be glory and dominion for ever and ever.   Amen."[3]

[1]Kay.   [2]Psa. 89.15, Roth.   [3]Rev. 1.5, 6.

CHAPTER 3

"REST IN THE LORD"

Psalm 37.7

If we trust we do not worry,
If we worry we do not trust.

WE all know what it is to be tempted to worry. Sometimes we keep it inside ourselves, and sometimes we let it out, but "it is a fret, whether . . . within or without."[1]

I shall never forget the day when I suddenly realized that not to be inwardly at rest in difficult times was really like saying, "Carest Thou not that we perish?" and that is what the writer of Proverbs calls fretting against the Lord,[2] and as the 37th Psalm says so truly, "tendeth only to evil-doing".[3] And we know it does. Any sort of unrest leads that way, and so the word is always, "Rest in the Lord, and wait patiently for Him." *v.* 7.

"Fret not thyself . . . Trust . . . Rest . . ."

[1]Lev. 13.55, R.V.   [2]Prov. 19.3.   [3]Psa. 37.8, R.V.

Psa. 3.2: *Many there be which say of my soul, There is no help for him in God.*

Have you ever been discouraged and distressed because of something people said, or the voices inside you said? Such people and such voices talk most when one is in trouble about something. "Many there be which say of my soul, There is no help for him in God." That was what the many said who were round about poor King David in a dark hour. But he turned to his God and told Him just what they were saying, and then he affirmed his faith, "But Thou, O Lord, art a shield for me; my glory, and the lifter up of mine head." *v.* 3.

We cannot use these words if we are pleasing ourselves in anything, and doing our own will, not our Lord's. In that case what the many say is only too true. There is no help for us in God while we are walking in any way of our own choice. But when all is clear between us and our Father, even if like David we are in trouble because of something we have done wrong in the past, then those words are not true. There *is* help for us in God. He is our shield, our glory, and the lifter up of our head, and we need not be afraid of ten thousands of people[1] — ten thousands of voices — for the Lord our God is our very present Help.

Twice in Psalms 3 and 4 we find David taking the unkind words of others and putting them into a prayer. It was the wisest thing he could have done with them. The alternative would have been either to brood over them, or to talk to others of them; but no, he turns like a child to his father, "Many say of my soul, There is no help for him in God." "Many say, How can we experience good?"[2]

This last "many say" will come home to some of us, I think. It was spoken, as the first was, in a difficult time, and it was a hopelessly discouraging word: Who will show us any good? How can we experience good? Everything is going wrong. There is no comfort anywhere. This is how those voices speak.

But David is not confounded. He refuses to be cast down, let the many say what they will. "Lord, lift Thou up the light of Thy countenance upon us."[3]   If only we can look up and meet His ungrieved countenance, what does anything matter?   And we *shall* experience good.   "The Lord is my light and my salvation; whom shall I fear? the Lord is the strength of my life; of whom shall I be afraid?"[4]

[1]*v*. 6.   [2]Psa. 4.6, Del.   [3]Psa. 4.6.   [4]Psa. 27.1.

Entangled Circumstances

Exod. 14.3: *Pharaoh will say . . . , They are entangled in the land, the wilderness hath shut them in.*

Sometimes when problems come up and we see no way through, or when souls we love seem entangled, we are tempted to think of what *Pharaoh* will say.   There can be no entanglement, the wilderness cannot possibly shut in anyone whom God is leading Home.   It has been said, "What we see as problems, God sees as solutions"; and what we have to do through the age-long minute before we see is to wait in peace and refuse to be hustled.   "Fear ye not, stand still," and sooner or later, ye shall "see the salvation of the Lord".[1]   There will be no entanglement.

And is it not comforting that the Lord Jesus knows beforehand what *Pharaoh* will say? so we need not pay the slightest attention to him, even if he does make discouraging remarks.   The last word is never with *Pharaoh*.   What is he "but a noise"?[2]   So let us trust and not be afraid.

[1]*v*. 13.   [2]Jer. 46.17.

Have you ever felt that some words in the Bible are too great to be taken for your own?   And yet at one time or

another you have rested your heart upon them. Was that a
kind of presumption? Had you any right to do so? May
you do so now? Some such thought came to me this
morning, and this answered it: *Remember the word unto
Thy servant, upon which Thou hast caused me to hope;*[1]
"wherein Thou hast caused me to put my trust", is the
Prayer Book version. Because Thou didst cause me to rest
my heart upon that word of Thine, I trust Thee to fulfil it.
It was not I who found it and chose it and rested upon it.
It was Thou who didst cause me to do it, and this action
of Thine is my assurance now.

Confirm to Thy servant that promise of Thine.[2] This is
the word for sad days, disappointed days. We did receive
a promise, perhaps about some soul, perhaps about ourselves. Let us not give up our hope, even though we do not
yet see its fulfilment.

I have the right to pray that prayer. Thy love in giving
me that word is my warrant. It is not presumption, then
— "I stand upon Thy merits; I know no other stand". I
stand upon what Thou hast done. Thou — not anything
of myself — Thou hast caused me to hope.

The prayer that follows came about one special soul, but
it can be used for anyone about whom we sought and
received (as we believe) a promise not yet fulfilled:

> Confirm, O Lord, that word of Thine,
>   That Heavenly word of certainty,
> Thou gavest it: I made it mine,
>   Believed to see.
>
> And yet I see not; he, for whom
>   That good word came in Thy great love,
> Is wandering still, and there is room
>   For fear to move.

O God of Hope, what though afar
  From all desire that wanderer seems,
Thy promise fails not; never are
  Thy comforts dreams.

[1]Psa. 119.49.   [2]*v*. 38, Kay.

Rom. 15.13: *Now the God of hope fill you with all joy and peace in believing, that ye may abound in hope, through the power of the Holy Ghost.*

This is a great word for us all. We need to be continually renewed in hope because, although there are always happy things happening, the devil does not forget us. Every now and then we are sharply reminded that he is either a roaring lion, walking about among us, seeking whom he may devour; or he is a serpent, the kind that does not shrink away when he hears us coming, but is quite ready to attack and shoot venom at us, as some snakes are said to do. And it is quite easy to become discouraged when some who might resist him do not, and do not even seem to want to do so. I often thank God that He is the God of hope.

It is also a great word for all who love enough to suffer when those who were trusted have disappointed us. Paul wrote it in one of his earlier letters. About thirteen years later he wrote his last letter. The space between those two letters was filled with experiences of joy and sorrow, most of which are unrecorded. Among these is a story which comes very close to all of us who have had much to do with souls.

We know Paul loved and trusted his children in the faith who had become his fellow-workers. Twice we find one of these mentioned in the loving list of names at the end of two of his letters.[1] Then there is silence. What pangs, what strivings, what prayers, filled that silent space? We are told nothing of them, but our hearts tell us what his heart went through before he wrote of that same one in his last letter, "Demas hath forsaken me, having loved this present world".[2]

And yet — and it is this that comes close to us — there is no weakening in that last letter, no discouragement, no whisper of loss of faith in others, no fear. "For God hath not given us the spirit of fear; but of power, and of love, and of a sound mind. . . . I know whom I have believed,"[3] the God, not of despondency, but of hope.

[1]Col. 4.14; Philem. 24.   [2]2 Tim. 4.10.   [3]2 Tim. 1.7, 12.

Psa. 63.8, Roth.: *My soul hath run clinging to Thee, on me hath Thy right hand laid hold.*

Rotherham's title to this Psalm calls it "A melody of David when he was in the wilderness". There may be private wildernesses appointed for one and another, and this is a good word for such times, because it came straight out of that very experience. We are safe if we run clinging; we are safe, for we are held. All we need is there. What a melody to come out of a wilderness!

Other versions of this verse are equally illuminating: "My soul hangeth upon Thee: Thy right hand hath upholden me."[1] "My soul has clung fast after Thee: Thy right hand has firm hold on me."[2] Kay's note is: "Problems, which occupied hundreds of controversial treatises, as to the relation of Divine grace and human will, have their solution in this one verse." Is it God who holds me, and so keeps me safe? or is it I who hold God and so am safe? The word of our Father shows both holds; it does not explain them, or reconcile them, or say which matters more; it just shows them and leaves us looking at both. Because we love Him and could do no other, "my soul hath run clinging to Thee." But not only that, "on me hath Thy right hand laid hold."

So we end with our eyes off ourselves and fixed on Him who has firm hold of us. To Him indeed be glory for ever and ever, Amen.

¹v. 9, P.B.V.   ²v. 8, Kay.

CHAPTER 4

"LORD, TEACH US TO PRAY"

Luke 11.1

SOMEBODY said once to me, "Does not God know what we need before we ask Him? Then why ask Him?"

But the Lord told us to ask, even though our Father knew what we needed. It is impossible to fight the Lord's battles without spending as much time as possible with our Commander, both alone and with others. Even to our Lord Jesus Christ the Father said, "*Desire of Me,* and I shall give Thee . . ."[1]

This is from *The Pilgrim's Progress*: The Reliever (who had greatly helped the Pilgrims in their distress) said, "I marvelled much . . . that you petitioned not the Lord for a Conductor".

Christiana said, "But since our Lord knew it would be for our profit, I wonder that He sent not one along with us!"

The Reliever answered, *"It is not always necessary to grant things not asked for . . . and it is a poor thing that is not worth asking for."*

"Desire of Me, and I shall give thee . . ."

[1]Psa. 2.8, P.B.V.

Distractions in prayer

Sometimes, when some distraction has called us off, we

45

cannot even remember for what we were praying. "Sometimes I finde that I had forgot what I was about, but when I began to forget I cannot tell." These words were written nearly 200 years ago, but they might have been written by some of us yesterday. "I pray giddily and circularly, and returne againe and againe to that I have said before, and perceive not that I do so."

"We have not an high priest which cannot be touched with the feeling of our infirmities",[1] and He has a gentle way of recalling us from these undesired wanderings.

I have found that it is fatal to get into a kind of hot fuss over our elusive thoughts. That is exactly what the adversary wants us to do. The only way is to refuse to chase about: "Be still, and know . . ."[2] "In quietness and in confidence shall be your strength",[3] for prayer as for all else. Often by a way so simple that a child can follow it, the tempter may be foiled.

Sometimes nothing helps so much as to turn from trying to pray, and instead, to read on the knees of the spirit some familiar passage from the Bible, for those words have a power in them to effect that of which they speak. Another sure way into peace is found in a literal obedience to Colossians 3.16. Turn a psalm or a hymn into prayer, read or repeat it aloud, for to speak to oneself deep down in one's heart, using words that one knows and loves, is often a wonderfully quickening thing to do, and nothing more quickly and gently leads one into the place of peace, where prayer is born.

But often there is a wrestle. A thousand invisible enemies will seem to fill the air and crowd between you and your Lord. Each of them has a stinging or depressing word. We shall be reminded of prayers to which no answers have come yet (or what we call answers), and told that it will make no difference whether we pray or not. We shall be shown our own dreadful nothingness so clearly that we shall hardly be able to bring ourselves to believe that such prayers as we can offer will rise to God at all. Our wrestling is with these whispering or shouting spiritual foes. We must press through, fight through, and the sword with which to fight is the blessed Word of God. Take, for example, that last keen thrust, our unworthiness; try on that the wonderful word in Revelation 8.3, 4, and press on: "And another angel came and stood at the altar, having a golden censer; and there was given unto him much incense, that he should offer it with the prayers of all saints upon the golden altar which was before the throne. And the smoke of the incense, which came with the prayers of the saints, ascended up before God out of the angel's hand."

[1]Heb. 4.15.   [2]Psa. 46.10.   [3]Isa. 30.15.

Sometimes we cannot find words. We are not always meant to find them. I have been greatly comforted in the word that says we are not heard for our much speaking.[1] We are not pledged to pour out words for half an hour. Words fail us at times. When Peter said, "Master, it is good for us to be here: and let us make three tabernacles", he seems to have spoken in a sort of hurry of spirit, "for he wist not what to say". And the answer to that rush of words was, "This is My beloved Son: hear Him."[2]

So do not be afraid of silence in your prayer time. It may be that you are meant to listen, not to speak. So wait before the Lord. Wait in stillness. Wait as David waited when he "sat before the Lord".[3] And in that stillness, assurance will come to you. You will know that you are heard; you will know that your Lord ponders the voice of your humble desires;[4] you will hear quiet words spoken to you yourself, perhaps to your grateful surprise and refreshment. And you will know that the power of your Lord will be great, "according as Thou hast spoken".[5]

[1]Matt. 6.7, 8.　　[2]Mark 9.5-7.　　[3]2 Sam. 7.18.
[4]Psa. 86.6, P.B.V.　　[5]Num. 14.17.

One of the greatest joys — perhaps the greatest — prepared for those who have yielded all to the Lord is that of learning to know their Lord and Leader in quite a new way. I am reading Abraham's life just now, and notice this: In Genesis 12 and 13 he makes new surrenders. In chapter 15 he has a wonderful time with God. (He falls more than once — the Bible is a true Book, and such things are not disguised — but he rises again and goes on.) In chapter 18 we have something that spoke to me anew today. We read of a meal under a tree. Our Lord Jesus Christ, two of His angels and Abraham meet and talk together. But then comes something more. The angels go away. "And Abraham drew near".[1] It is not enough to meet our Lord with others. We must meet Him alone. He has something more for us. What do I know of this?

[1]v. 23.

Exod. 17.12: *And his hands were steady until the going down of the sun.*

That is the kind of prayer that is much assaulted. Moses' hands were heavy. So are ours often, and we are very apt to lean on Aaron and Hur to hold them up, in other words, to depend on others to help us by their earnestness and steadfastness.   There is something kindling to prayer in being with others who are praying, and all through the Bible this is recognized — even in Gethsemane our dear Lord seems to have wanted human companionship in prayer. But He pressed through that sense of need as He must have done often before, and He can give it to us to press through. He can teach us more than we have yet learned of "access with confidence";[1] He can draw us deep into His own blessed Presence, even as He drew many a man of old — and among them was Moses — and He can strengthen our hands so that they shall be steady until the going down of the sun.

[1]Eph. 3.12.

Jonah 2.7: *When my soul fainted within me I remembered the Lord.*
Deut. 20.3: *Let not your hearts faint.*
Gal. 6.9: *In due season we shall reap, if we faint not.*
Luke 18.1, Weym.: *He also taught them by a parable that they must always pray and never lose heart.*

True access and communion with the Lord are not lightly obtained.   There is nothing ever lightly won where the deep things of the Spirit are concerned.   I can remember a whole day spent in what seemed utterly vain pressing through the thick, thick veils of time and sense and self before at last there was a break, and a word in my Bible became life to me.   But that word has lived for me ever since.   It is not the same for all.   I suppose the more perfectly we live in His Presence the more quickly we shall be aware of Him, and the more clearly we shall hear Him; but I do know that

at any time we may be tested by disappointment, and need
to ask God to give us persistence. And He will not refuse.
He understands. He has told us that He does. And in the
end — oh, joy of all joys — we shall hear the Voice we
love best in all the world saying to us, even to us, "I know
. . . how thou hast not fainted."

Mark 8.23: *If thou canst believe, all things are possible to
him that believeth.*

"All things"? It is a tremendous word. This morning I
was praying for one who sorely needs the miracle of a great
deliverance, and I found myself praying the prayer-chorus
written for such hours:

> O blessed God of Hope,
>   Flow through me *mightily*
> Until I hope for everyone
> As Thou hast hoped for me.

We need the *patience* of hope, and so that verse, as first
written, was "Flow through me *patiently*", but there are
times when we need to pray for a *mighty* renewal of hope,
hope that like a great wave will sweep up and carry all
our fears and doubts before it. "Hope through me, hope
of God".

Gen. 18.14: *Is any thing too hard for the Lord?*

I have heard this word used as a plea in asking for something very much desired which appeared to be for the glory
of God. But I think we sometimes forget that the question

refers to something God had said was to happen. It was not that Abraham said, "Lord, do such and such things for me. Surely they would be for Thy glory? Is any thing too hard for the Lord?" but that God Himself was speaking of something which He had appointed to be. (See Gen. 17.16-19.)

Again and again I have been saved from disappointment in prayer by remembering this.

Jer. 32.27: *Behold, I am the Lord, the God of all flesh: is there any thing too hard for Me?*

God had told Jeremiah to do a very difficult thing. The armies of the Chaldeans were round about the city of Jerusalem, and they were going to take it, and yet He told His servant to buy a field, just as though everything was going well. And Jeremiah had obeyed. He was in prison at the time, but God never gives a command without making obedience possible (see verses 6, 7, 8). Then, having obeyed, he feels free to tell his God all his perplexities.

And God answers him. He does not explain anything, but He does answer him with words of peace. He has the whole situation in His hands. He is not baffled even by Israel's failure. He will perfect that which concerneth them. "Is there any thing too hard for Me?"

I have often heard these two questions of the Lord's, and also Jeremiah's "There is nothing too hard for Thee," used in prayer; and as I said before, used about something greatly desired which seemed to be for the glory of God. Sometimes there is something in the Bible which would direct our thinking if only we considered it. Sometimes there is something in the circumstances which God appoints, which will show us — if we are living near enough to Him to understand His wishes — what we may, and what we may not, ask. Again there are times when He speaks to us and says to us, as He did to St. Paul, Not this that you desire, but something which will help others more, is My gift to you. Be content with that. (See 2 Cor. 12.7-10.)

Some have been puzzled because good things earnestly prayed for have not been given. What is happening is quite a different kind of answer. We do not feel like calling it wonderful. We feel like calling it disappointing. And yet we know that it would not have been allowed to happen if it had been, what it looks like, simply a calamity. "I know the plans which I am planning for you, plans of welfare and not of calamity, to give you a future and a hope."[1] These words are true, however things appear; and faith lays hold upon them, and refuses to be discouraged. The thoughts of our God are thoughts of peace and not of evil. So even now, let us trust and not be afraid. This will discomfit the devil and glorify our God.

[1]Jer. 29.11, Roth.

Sometimes people speak of God having answered their prayer, but what they mean is that He has answered it according to their desire and done something about which they are glad. If He does something different they say sadly, "He has not answered." All this is a mistake. Prayer is always heard if the one who prays comes to the Father in the Name of our Lord Jesus. "I love the Lord, because He hath heard"[1] can be our word always, and also that other word, "This is the confidence that we have in Him, that, if we ask any thing according to His will, He heareth us: and if we know that He hear us, whatsoever we ask, we know that we have the petitions that we desired of Him."[2]   If we love Him, our real prayer is that His perfect will may be done, whatever the words are, and so it is certain that we have the petition even before we see it granted.   The form the answer takes does not affect the fact.

I know that sometimes we do not see how the thing granted is at all what we desire.   And yet it is (I write for His lovers only).   For, after all, what the deepest in us wanted was not our own natural will, but the will of our Father.   So what is given *is* our hearts' desire; He hath not withholden the request of our lips.[3]   *But God always answers us in the deeps, never in the shallows of our soul:* in hours of confusion, it can help to remember this.

[1]Psa. 116.1.   [2]Jn. 5.14, 15.   [3]Psa. 21.2.

Matt. 18.19:   *Again I say unto you, That if two of you shall agree on earth as touching any thing that they shall ask, it shall be done for them of My Father which is in Heaven.*

Sometimes two have agreed on earth as touching something which they asked.   With special earnestness they asked for it.   And looking on from outside, people would say that it was not given to them.   But is that true?   What did they really ask?   Surely their deepest prayer was, "Do what is most for Thy glory."   We know, because our Lord has said it, that no prayer is unheard, unanswered.   So that special and earnest prayer must have been heard and answered. The answer to such prayers is never "No".   The Father does what He sees is most to His glory.   It is there that faith comes in, for we do not see how it can be for His glory.   But then, after all, we are counted on to walk by

faith, not by sight. Perhaps we have prayed for the recovery of one who was ill, and that one did not recover.
What was our heart's desire for that one? Recovery?
Surely our deepest desire was that the Father's blessed will should be done and His Name glorified.

It is a great comfort in tempted hours to turn from all that seems to be, and to believe that the prayer of the "two" (and the many) was answered and will be answered however impossible it may seem. The loving Father of those who prayed would never disappoint His beloved children. I wonder if that was Paul's comfort sometimes, when the prayers of his friends brought not the expected answer but another quite different, which, as we can all see now, was the real answer to their deepest prayer.

Perhaps there are other things about which you have prayed, and yet those things have not been given. Let my comfort be yours. If your prayer at its deepest was not for what you wanted, but for what He, whom you love best, saw to be most for His glory, then your prayer is answered.
You cannot see how? Never mind. He sees how. Is that not enough?

"Delight thyself also in the Lord; and He shall give thee the desires of thine heart." Psa. 37.4.

Rest — *to rest again.* Matt. 11.28.
Rest — *a ceasing.* Matt. 11.29.
Rest — *to rest down, or thoroughly.* Heb. 4.8.

"He that is entered into his rest, he also hath ceased from his own works.... Let us labour therefore to enter into that rest".[1] And *labour* here means "make haste". Is the word used to remind us that we shall not drift into rest?

There must be the will to enter in, and perhaps the thing demanding most will is the resolution to cease from our own works (Young translates it *business* — the busy traffic of our thoughts) and stay our minds upon our God.

I have found succour in these words in St. Matthew and in Hebrews. For many years it has been so, or long ago I should have been overborne. So I commend them to all who are tried in this or any way which pertains to the unexplained, as opening a door into peace. The discovery of the meaning of the words translated *rest,* as given in Young, has only emphasized that which has been my strong consolation a thousand times.

We pray: the answer is not what we expect. It seems an answer of loss, and sometimes loss upon loss. We must cease from our own thoughts about it, and, while holding our prayer before our God, believe that what is allowed to be contains the perfect answer for the moment; and we rest down, we rest thoroughly; the sense of strain has passed in peace.

And this covers all life — illness of those we love, mental or spiritual suffering, strange turns of the road, the unexplained, everything, everywhere.

Let us not lose one hour in needless, ineffective distress; let us hasten by an act of the will (by God's enabling) to enter into His rest, to come to Him for rest, to rest again.

[1]Heb. 4.10, 11.

I have never noticed till lately that the Letter that opens the door into Heaven gives us a most beautiful illustration of what life can be if we walk through that door and sit in Heavenly places in Christ. For surely 2 Corinthians 4.16-18 and 2 Corinthians 12.7-10 are so connected.

I suppose there is nothing Satan tries oftener to use to our undoing than the answer to a prayer that does not look like an answer at all. Among all the things which are seen, it is the one that can try us most. It is sometimes so entirely unexplained, and so very undesired. Children, who do not know their Father very well, call it an unanswered prayer — it puzzles them so much that they think of it like that. But we must not. We shall lose great treasure if we do. Let us help each other not to do so.

If St. Paul had thought that his prayer was unanswered; if he had not caught the words of the answer; recognized the opportunity that would never come again, and shared the whole story in the love of his heart with his friends who were living in difficult Corinth; above all, if he had not lived in the light of the Heavenly words that he heard — how much we should have missed. And if he could have looked down the ages and seen the golden gain that was to come to his Lord through this single incident, would he not have sung? He did not see, but he did sing, "Therefore I take pleasure in infirmities . . . for when I am weak, then am I strong" — wonderful words. Verily, "the things which are seen are temporal; but the things which are not seen are eternal."

I have had Acts 21.4 in mind for years as one of the most difficult verses in the whole Bible. Rotherham translates it thus: "They unto Paul began to say through the Spirit, that he would gain no footing in Jerusalem." The chief message of this chapter to me is this, that we must be willing to let those we love go up to Jerusalem. We must be inwardly willing. I do not find this easy. Human love wants to shelter and to spare; Divine love is braver. Lord, evermore give us this love.

O Father, help, lest our poor love refuse
For our beloved the life that they would choose,
And in our fear of loss for them, or pain,
    Forget eternal gain.

Show us the gain, the golden harvest there
For corn of wheat that they have buried here;
Lest human love defraud them and betray,
    Teach us, O God, to pray.

Teach us to pray, remembering Calvary,
For as the Master must the servant be;
We see their face set toward Jerusalem,
    Let us not hinder them.

Teach us to pray; O Thou who didst not spare
Thine own Beloved, lead us on in prayer;
Purge from the earthly, give us love Divine,
    Father, like Thine, like Thine.

From prayer that asks that I may be
Sheltered from winds that beat on Thee
. . . O Lamb of God deliver me.

As I thought of this prayer, the "I" changed to "they",
and I found it a far more piercing word. I was not sure
that I could pray meaning it to the full.

Then I thought of the angels watching our Lord Jesus as
He walked the roads of the earth, beaten by winds — and
what bitter winds — did they ever come to the Father with
pitiful prayers for His shelter? Would they have made it
harder for that Father (I speak in human language) by

asking Him to do what He could not do without eternal
loss to His beloved Son and the souls that He had made?

Let us learn to pray on earth as they pray in Heaven.
"Fashion our mortal speech that we may know to pray the
Heavenly way."

John 12.20-28.

The coming of the Greeks "heralded the proclamation of
the Gospel to the Gentiles. For this the Passion and the
Resurrection were the necessary conditions." Westcott's
note, as always, opens into wide countries of thought. "The
glory of the Son of man lay in the bringing to Himself of
all men by the Cross (*v.* 32), and rising through death
above death. In this victory over death by death there is
the complete antithesis to the Greek view of life, in which
death was hidden."

This leads on into the wonderful word about the corn of
wheat which is "separated from all in which it had lived
before." And that leads to yet another word which needs
to be read on the knees of the spirit: "Now is My soul
troubled; and what shall I say? Father, save Me from this
hour: but for this cause came I unto this hour. Father,
glorify Thy name."

These words have been understood in two opposite ways.
This is Westcott's way: "The petition is for deliverance *out
of,* and not for deliverance *from,* the crisis of trial. So
that the sense appears to be 'bring me safely *out of* the
conflict', and not simply 'keep me *from* entering into it.' "
And he understands "But" to mean, "Nay, this I need not
say: the end is know."

As I read the verses that come before this prayer, it

seemed to me that our Lord Jesus was not thinking only of Himself and His conflict (was it ever His way to think only of Himself?), but of all His followers who would accept the law of the corn of wheat, yes, even of the least of them. He would know how, to many, by far the bitterest death would be to see their dearest die, whether in the swift death of martyrdom or in the long death of a life laid down for the brethren. And here, as always, He shows the way. For the very young and the weak, and for the suffering, there may be the prayer that shelters, but nowhere in the Bible do I find sheltering prayer for comrades in the fight.

> O loving Comforter, help our infirmities,
> That which we know not teach;
> Fashion our mortal speech
> That we may know to pray
> Our Saviour's way.

Matt. 26.39: *O My Father, if it be possible, let this cup pass from Me.*

Luke 22.42: *Father, if Thou be willing, remove this cup from Me.*

(From = away from, as compared with John 12.27, from = out of.)

Westcott says somewhere that in his study of the New Testament he had come to feel that the very tenses of the verbs were inspired. Surely inspiration, and nothing less, accounts for this: In the three records of our Lord's prayer in Gethsemane we find the word our human hearts naturally use, the "from" that means *away from,* not the "from" that means *out of.* "And He went forward a little, and fell on the ground, and prayed that, if it were possible, the hour might pass from Him.   And He said, Abba, Father, all things are possible unto Thee; take away this cup from Me: nevertheless not what I will, but what Thou wilt."[1]

Is there not infinite comfort here?   "We have not an high priest which cannot be touched with the feeling of our infirmities; but was in all points tempted like as we are, yet without sin."[2]   I think that verse finds perfect illustration in the prayer that shows us His natural will blended with His Father's will — the "away from" is balanced by "if it be possible" and "nevertheless not My will but Thine be done".   Then was the prayer of John 12.27 answered, for He was delivered *out of* though not *away from;* and using what I think of as our own hearts' word, He came close to our hearts.   He comes close to them now, saying, "My child, I have been there; I understand."

When St. Paul prayed to be delivered from the impaling stake ("thorn" is far too weak a word) that the messenger of Satan was driving through his being, he used the word meaning *away from* not *out of.*   "For this thing I besought the Lord thrice, that it might depart from me."   But after our Lord had answered him in the glorious words that have been strength and comfort to the tried all down the ages, he rose to the heights: "Most gladly therefore will I rather glory in my infirmities, that the power of Christ may rest upon me."[3]   That seems to me to be the very mountain peak of triumphant life.   Oh, to live there; Lord, give it to us to live there.

> "I wish to have no wishes left,
>   But to leave all to Thee;
> And yet I wish that Thou should'st will
>   Things that I wish should be."

Faber wrote that long ago. We all know how true it is. The poem goes on to say, "But, Lord! I have a death to die, and not a death to choose", and these words have often changed the current of my desires. He who made Paul the valorous man he was; He who brought him through the *away from* attitude towards his devastating buffeting, led him into the *out of* life, made him more than conqueror — He is with us here. What He did, He can do. "I will trust, and not be afraid."[4]

[1]Mark 14.35, 36.   [2]Heb. 4.15.   [3]2 Cor. 12.7-9.   [4]Isa. 12.2.

The other day a note came to me which was such a cup of cold water that I cannot keep it to myself. Many of you know the rendering which it quotes, but even to such it may come with the blessed freshness and power that distinguishes the words of God from all other words, and to others it will be new: "Yes, and His Spirit too — for His compassion matches our yearning — is ever taking our human frailty by the hand. *We* are not even sure what boons should rightly be the object of our prayers; but His Spirit — His very Spirit — is pleading ever for us with sighings such as no language can shape into words. Ah, but He who tracks the labyrinth of the heart needs no words to divine what the Spirit means: He knows that His Spirit intercedes for His hallowed ones in just the way that God desires."[1]

Sometimes in prayer we seem to get beyond the sphere of words, but "He who tracks the labyrinth of the heart needs no words", and He takes "our human frailty by the hand", and leads us in the path of prayer.

Perhaps some may feel, "But I never go deep enough into prayer to get beyond the sphere of words — I never lose myself in prayer. My difficulties are quite different."

It helps me very much to remember that "human frailty" includes every kind of difficulty, even the difficulty of wandering thoughts, which is, I think, the chief of all the hindrances to prayer. And when we cannot pray as we long to do, then (so this wonderful verse tells us) the Spirit prays for us, "in just the way that God desires."

Is not this a comfort? When we are distressed because we have failed to pray as we meant to do and longed to do; when we are tired, and seem unable to fix our thoughts steadily on anything; when we are puzzled, and do not know what we should ask for; when we feel too sinful to draw near and pray at all — then the Compassion of our Father takes us by the hand, and the Blood of Jesus Christ His Son cleanses us from all sin, and the Loving Spirit leads us forth into the land of prayer; and if, even then, we cannot pray ourselves, He prays for us "in just the way that God desires."

[1]Rom. 8.26, 27, Way.

Rev. 8.3, 4. *Much Incense.*

I have been finding heart-comfort in the *Much Incense* that is offered with our poor prayers, connecting it with the "golden bowls full of incense, which are the prayers of the saints."[1] It is a wonderful word, and there is something so delightful in what follows, "And they sing a new song" — prayer and praise mingle here. So we follow a Heavenly pattern in our services of mingled prayer and song. But when we think of the more intimate aspects of prayer, some of us must feel, as I do, very much at the edge of things.

But just here He meets us, our wonderful understanding Lord, for chapter 8 comes after chapter 5. We are not told of the Much Incense until our souls are hungry for a reassuring word. "And another angel came and stood at the altar, having a golden censer; and there was given unto him *much incense,* that he should offer it with the prayers of all saints upon the golden altar which was before the throne. And the smoke of the incense, which came with the prayers of the saints, ascended up before God out of the angel's hand." Happy angel, his is indeed a ministry of comfort.

Week by week, always on Saturday evening as a preparation, I suppose, for the worship of Sunday, the dear old man who was as a father to me (and to the Keswick Convention)* used to pray, "We thank Thee, O Saviour, for the Much Incense of Thy merits"; and the phrase sank deep into my mind, and all these years has stayed with me. What should we do if there were no Much Incense?

But today something new to me fills me with wonder. That precious Much Incense is offered just as our poor prayers are; there is no difference made. Both are offered in golden vessels — the one a bowl, the other a censer, but both of gold. It is as though the very imagery of Heaven were called upon to tell us, to *assure* us, that what we feel is too utterly unworthy to be offered is so dear to our God that He has it brought to Him in a golden censer.

[1]Rev. 5.8, 9, R.V.

Many may be tempted to think, "What difference will it make whether I pray or not?" Remember that your prayer — even yours, even mine — has power because it is offered in the Name that is above every name; the Name of our Lord Jesus gives force to the prayer of the tiniest child.

*Robert Wilson.

In times like these in which we are living,* all sensitive souls feel the influences of what the Bible calls the smoke from the bottomless pit.[1] It is possible to be smothered by it and weakened in the spiritual fight to which we are called. I have been living lately in the first part of Revelation 17.14: "These shall make war with the Lamb, and the Lamb shall overcome them: for He is Lord of lords, and King of kings".

"There are no neutral hearts except those that have stopped beating: there are no neutral prayers" — I have just now read this in a paper that has been sent to me. It is the whisper of the tempter which suggests that it is no use to pray. Do not let us listen to him. Continually, when the news of world events would cast me down, I find new life in remembering two great scriptures. One is the story of the temptation of our Lord. The devil dared not have offered to do what he could not do; he must have known that the Lord Jesus would instantly recognize the deception. The fact that he *could* give the kingdoms of the world to one who put himself in his power by worshipping him made his offer what it was, a real temptation. We have seen what happens when a man does what our Lord refused to do. One by one the kingdoms are given to him. This scripture opens a window on present-day history. Looking through it we understand, as we could not do otherwise, what lies behind all that we read and hear.

The other great scripture to which I turn is the story of the Crucifixion. Have you ever taken time to ponder what it meant to the Father, the Holy Spirit, and the angels to wait through those awful hours while the Beloved of high

*This and the following paragraphs were written during the Second World War.

Heaven hung on the Cross? But those hours had an end. "He said, It is finished: and He bowed His head...."[2]

These hours, months, years, will have an end. Those who have not been neutral in their prayers through this long agony will share in the solemn joy of His triumph, when a voice, which all hell cannot subdue, says, "It is done."[3] May God give us to burn with a steady white-hot heat, never for one hour to be neutral in our prayers till His purpose is accomplished, and those who have imagined a vain thing know the meaning of the scorching words in the Psalm, "He that sitteth in the heavens shall laugh".[4]

[1]Rev. 9.1, 2.   [2]Jn. 19.30.   [3]Rev. 21.6.   [4]Psa. 2.4.

CHAPTER 5

"A NEW SONG IN MY MOUTH"
Psalm 40.3

THREE verses taken together help to show the life of thanksgiving we are meant to live:

(1) Psa. 40.2, 3, P.B.V.: *He . . . ordered my goings. And He hath put a new song in my mouth: even a thanksgiving unto our God.* A new song for a new occasion. Today gives us a new occasion. I think it must please our God when we offer a new song, even a thanksgiving to Him who orders our goings.

(2) Heb. 13.15: *Let us offer the sacrifice of praise to God continually, . . . giving thanks to His Name.* "Continually" means continually, not off and on, not only when we are doing what we would choose to do, not just when there are no "if only"s buzzing about us like flies. So it means today, all through the day, every day, right on to the end.

(3) Psa. 118.14, Roth.: *My might and melody is the Lord.* Isn't that beautiful? and Kay goes on, "And He is become my salvation." What a God, what a Book! Every verse is a jewel-mine.

Sometimes it is a help to remember that we are not the only people who have been tempted to be cast down. "For if I be cast down, they that trouble me will rejoice at it"[1] is as true now as ever it was. But look at the words that follow: "My trust is in Thy mercy: and my heart is joyful in Thy salvation. I will sing of the Lord, because He hath dealt so lovingly with me: yea, I will praise the Name of the Lord most Highest." That is where we are meant to live, and where we can live, if we will. There is no provision in the whole Bible for a despondent Christian. "Thanks be unto God, which always causeth us to triumph in Christ"[2] — that is the word for us all.

[1]Psa. 13.4, P.B.V.   [2]2 Cor. 2.14.

1 Thess. 5.18: *In every thing give thanks.*

This is a constant word to me. It is so easy to give thanks for what one naturally chooses, but that does not cover the "every thing" of the text.

I have read of John Bunyan making a flute of the leg of his stool. When his jailer came to stop him playing on this queer flute, he slipped it back in its place in his stool. The joy of the Lord is an unquenchable thing. It does not depend upon circumstances, or upon place, or upon health (though health is a tremendous help to joy), or upon our being able to do what we want to do. It is like our river. It has its source high up among the mountains, and the little happenings down in the river-bed do not affect it.

One morning lately, in speaking of some small trouble, I quoted, "In every thing give thanks", and at once someone answered, "But I cannot give thanks for everything." Now, if our God tells us to do a thing and we say cannot, there is something wrong somewhere, for we all know the words, "I can do all things through Christ which strengtheneth me"[1] — that is, all things commanded. It is treason to say, "I cannot." But first we should make sure that

we are commanded to do this that we feel we cannot do.
I do not think we are anywhere told to give thanks *for*
everything. To make sure of this verse which is sometimes
quoted with "for" instead of "in", I looked it up in seven
versions. In six of the seven it is *in;* one version only has
for. So I take it that we may understand the word to mean,
not "Give thanks *for* everything", but "Give thanks *in*
everything", which is a different matter. All God's biddings
are enablings. We can do that. *We will do that.*

This is Way's rendering of Ephesians 5.20: "Speak out
your thoughts to each other in psalms, in hymns, in chants
inspired by the Holy Spirit. Let the sound of your singing,
let the music of your hearts go up to the Lord in unceasing
thanksgiving for all that He sends you." It is a singing
word. I take it as definitely that, and not as a direction
to give thanks for wrong things, the sinful actions that cause
Him grief, the pain of the world, and so on. In the midst
of all these things we are to give thanks — *in,* not *for.*
Here in writing to the Ephesians St. Paul uses another word
which Bishop Moule translates "over", but Way's rendering
makes the meaning clear. We are trusted to use our common sense (His gift) in reading our Bibles; for example,
when we are told to rejoice in all that we put our hands
to,[2] it obviously means right things, not wrong. So we need
not be troubled or puzzled because we cannot give thanks
for certain things that happen, things that we know grieve
our Lord. How could we? but knowing that all things work
together for good — yes, even these things — we can give
thanks in the thick of them. For He shall reign, and all
things shall be compelled to minister to His glory.

I have been thinking today of St. Paul and of how he

certainly did not consider examination by torture a thing for which to give thanks (if he had he would not have used means to avoid it); and yet when he had to suffer, we know what he did. The story in Acts 16.22-25 is an eternal reminder of what we are all meant to be and do. We are *not* meant to be fair-weather Christians; we are never promised fair weather.

Down in the midst of the storm and the darkness, "on every hand hard-pressed am I — yet not crushed", "in many-sided endurance"[3] — yet in spirit lifted above it all. In it, yet in Christ first. He is nearer, more truly round us, than the encompassing circumstances. Is it not wonderful? Let us pray for one another that we may live this life and never for a day be satisfied with anything less triumphant.

[1]Phil. 4.13.   [2]Deut. 12.7.   [3]2 Cor. 4.8; 6.4, Way.

Heb. 12.28, Weym.: *Let us cherish thankfulness.*

I think thankfulness is like a flower. It needs care and cherishing if it is to live and grow. Perhaps thankfulness, even more than some other qualities that seem to come naturally to us, is in need of cherishing, because of the withering winds of life.

The best way to cause it to grow strong in our hearts is to be careful never to let ourselves be *un*thankful. Has anyone done anything to help me and I have said nothing about it? (It is not enough to thank God; we should thank the one to whom He gave the loving thought that caused the loving deed.) Has anyone prepared a surprise for me and I have been blind to it? or if I noticed it, have I been dumb? If we have been careless about this, let us put it right. I often think we must disappoint our kind Father by not noticing the little things (as well as the countless great things) that He does to give us pleasure. Perhaps we should begin by thinking more of what His children do for love of Him and for love of us too.

As I read in Hebrews I came upon a cause for very great thankfulness that I had not noticed before. Suppose the Old Testament promises were only for those to whom they were first given; suppose we had no right to take them to ourselves (some say this is so), what a tremendous loss it would be. Hebrews 13.5 was the word that brought this home to me just now. There we have the essence of three glorious verses from the Old Testament (and another in the next verse) from scriptures of truth and comfort belonging to other people, given to us for our own use. I take it that the Spirit of God guided the writer of Hebrews, both in the choice of his quotations and in the translation of them, so that we have the very words which can help us most. "I will in no wise fail thee, neither will I in any wise forsake thee"[1] from Genesis 28.15, Deuteronomy 31.6, 8, Joshua 1.5; and then, "The Lord is my helper; I will not fear: what shall man do unto me?"[1] from Psalm 118.6, and see Psalm 56.9-13.

What can man, or devil, or my own self do to me, if I may truly know that the Lord of Heaven and earth is my helper, and that He truly says to me, "I will in no wise fail thee, neither will I in any wise forsake thee"?

So let us *cherish thankfulness.* "In God's word will I rejoice: in the Lord's word will I comfort me."[2] For though my soul is among lions every day of its life, with me is the most high God that shall perform the cause which I have in hand.[3]

---

[1]R.V.   [2]Psa. 56.10, P.B.V.   [3]Psa. 57.4, 2, P.B.V.

Psa. 137.3, P.B.V.:   *Melody in our heaviness.*

I do not think that such heaviness as was felt by the people who were led captive into Babylon is meant to be lightened by melody; but there is another kind of heaviness, the tired-out feeling that may come, and that our Lord knew when He sat on the well.[1] I am quite sure that sometimes this kind of heaviness has to be. If it were not so, we should not know how to help other tired people. These words, "melody in our heaviness", show us one of the quickest ways out of the heaviness that depresses the spirit, even though all may be clear between us and our Lord. Try melody — try singing. If you cannot sing aloud, sing in your heart — "singing and making melody in your heart to the Lord".[2]

Sometimes we cannot sing much, but we can look up to our God and say a word or two. I did not know till one day last week that He calls that little word a song. In the Revised Version of Psalm 42.8 we have this: "In the night His song shall be with me, even a prayer unto the God of my life." (Other versions have the same thought — *prayer is song to God.*)

"If thou be tempted, rise thou on the wings of prayer to thy Beloved", and He will take that poor little prayer and turn it into a song.

From the midst of frustrations in Central Africa, Fred Arnot, who was the Livingstone of those regions, wrote, "I am learning never to be disappointed, but to praise."

I read that journal letter of his when it came home — it must be more than forty years ago — but that vital word in an ordinary letter remained with me ready for a moment of need. *I am learning never to be disappointed, but to praise.* God keep us so near to Himself that there will

be little shining seeds like that scattered about our letters —
seeds that will bear harvests of joy somewhere, sometime,
and be melody to others in their heaviness.

¹Jn. 4.6.   ²Eph. 5.19.

Psalm 28.6-9.

These verses are strong food. We have the jubilant
seventh verse: "In Him hath trusted my heart and I have
found help, therefore hath my heart danced for joy, and
with my song do I praise Him." (Roth.) And then immediately, "The Lord is their strength, and He is a strong-
hold of salvation" (R.V.); and in the last verse of the
Psalm Rotherham has, "Tend them also and carry them,
unto times age-abiding."

What helped me was the understanding of our human
weakness. The Psalmist does not say, I have received such
help that my heart danced for joy, and in the strength of
that glorious memory I shall go on to the end: but he
recognizes what is absolute truth, that whatever the Lord
has been to us in the past, we need Him as much as ever
today, and shall need Him on to the end. We may have
been so happy that we sang songs, but we cannot live on
our songs, nor on any other joy, not even on the joy that
He has given in the past.

Feed us then, O Bread of Life. Tend us also and carry
us, and let us dwell between Thy shoulders for ever.

Luke 24.51, 52: *He was parted from them . . . and they . . . returned to Jesusalem with great joy.*

I have often said that there is nothing in the Scriptures to encourage us to live the life that has what it desires, and frets if it cannot have it. There is no provision made for a life of that kind. Always we are expected to live triumphantly without what we would naturally wish for most; and full provision is made for that kind of life. The words quoted above show this perfectly. He whom they most desired, He whose preciousness they understood as they never had before, was parted from them, "and they worshipped Him, and returned to Jesusalem [where any day they might have to suffer for His sake] with great joy: and were *continually* in the temple [not weakened by longings for what they could not have, but] praising and blessing God."

Psa. 13.6, P.B.V.: *I will sing of the Lord, because He hath dealt so lovingly with me: yea, I will praise the Name of the Lord most Highest.*

Such words of joy are like sluice-gates. Open them and floods pour through, floods of memories of a love which "hath dealt so lovingly" with us; floods of reasons for being sure that it will be so to the end. It would be as impossible to think of these memories and reasons one by one, as it would be to separate the water-floods into separate drops; but two single drops from the great flood refreshed me this morning: "Thou maintainest [upholdest] my lot."[1] So it is as though a hand gathered up the minutes of this new day, before ever it begins, as one might gather up a handful of pearls, and all that the day is going to mean is upheld from minute to minute. "Thou art maintaining my lot" is Rotherham's word, so that all is well for today. And for tomorrow: "As for me, I will behold Thy face in righteousness: I shall be satisfied, when I awake, with Thy likeness";[2] or, as Rotherham has it, "I . . . shall be satisfied when awakened by a vision of Thee."

[1]Psa. 16.5.　　[2]Psa. 17.15.

CHAPTER 6

"THINK IT NOT STRANGE"

1 Peter 4.12

All that grieves is but for a moment;
All that pleases is but for a moment;
Only the Eternal is important.

MOST of you know these words; I want to remind you of
them. The Eternal in anything is the unseen, the spiritual.
A trial comes. It will pass. In a few days, or months, or
years, we shall have forgotten it. The way we meet that
trial — our inner attitude towards it — belongs to the things
that are eternal. It will matter ten thousand years hence
whether we conquered or were conquered by that temptation
to impatience or faithlessness or worry which came when
the trial rushed upon us.

It does not seem so now. We feel, "If only I could
have *that* — that joy on which my heart is set — then I
should be happy." But these words remind us of something
we know is true, and yet often forget. The pleasure will
pass. There is nothing abiding in pleasure, but there is
something abiding in our attitude towards that pleasure. If
we say, "I must have it; I shall not be happy if I cannot
have it", then even if we did have it, there would be no
lasting gain, only a dreadful loss, eternal loss.

There is a verse about this in the Bible: "He gave them

75

their request; but sent leanness into their soul."[1] Let us ask that this word may never be true of us.

[1]Psa. 106.15.

I have been reading Luke 1. "With God *nothing* shall be impossible."[1] Then I read Acts 12. James was killed in prison; Peter was set free. God, with whom nothing is impossible, did not answer the prayers of those who loved James in the same way as He answered the prayers of those who loved Peter. He could have done so, but He did not. "And blessed is he, whosoever shall not be offended in Me."[2] The words seem to me to be written across Acts 12. John must have wondered why the angel was not sent to James, or at least have been tempted to wonder. Again and again in Acts the Lord Jesus seems to say those words under His breath, as it were. Let us turn all our puzzles, all our temptations to wonder why, into opportunities to receive the blessing of the unoffended.

And now all the grief of those days has been utterly forgotten by those who loved James; they have all been together with him in the Presence of their Lord for 1900 years, and the one thing that matters now is how they lived through those days when their faith was tried to the uttermost.

So it will be with any who are longing to see the answer to their prayers for those who are in affliction, or any other adversity. In a few years — how few we do not know, but few at most — we shall all be together in joy. So with us, too, all that matters is how we live through these days while we are trusted to trust.

[1]v. 37.   [2]Luke 7.23.

Num. 31.23: *Every thing that may abide the fire, ye shall make it go through the fire, and it shall be clean.*

Is it not a tremendous comfort that a test of any sort proves that our God knows the soul can stand the test? Things that could not stand the fire were to be put into water — a much less fierce test of the stuff of which the thing was made. Our God is as tender with souls as with things. He will not put us through the fire unless He knows that we can "abide the fire".

Is anyone being tempted now because of some new call to deny utterly that *I* which so delights to rise up within us? Does the trial of patience or good temper, or of the loyal obedience which is the hallmark of discipline seem very fiery? Take hope, and sing a song of joy to Him for that He counted you faithful, putting you into the ministry[1] — the service which asks this denial of self from you. Thank Christ Jesus our Lord for *that*.

[1] Tim. 1.12.

Matt. 8.23-27; Mark 4.35-41; Luke 8.22-25.

The first word that spoke to me in this story was, "Behold, there arose a great tempest in the sea, insomuch that the ship was covered with the waves". The Lord Jesus was in the midst of that tempest with His disciples, so He understands when we are beset by tempests. He understands. He knows that the trials of our faith are not little things to us. *He knows* — that was what helped.

The next word was, "But He was asleep." "He was in the hinder part of the ship, asleep on a pillow". "As they sailed He fell asleep". The calm, the quietness, of those words rested me in a way I cannot describe. The ship may be covered with waves, fears may cover one's heart, like waves washing over it and chilling all within it; but if *He* be there, and at rest in our midst, what does it matter? "Why are ye fearful?" — that is His word always. "Why are ye so fearful?" "Where is your faith?" If *He* sees no reason for fear, why should we?

Perhaps this will find someone fearing about something. "Master, carest Thou not?" He cares. "And He . . . said unto the sea, Peace, be still."

Sometimes there are special tests like illness, trial of various kinds, a disappointment, more than usually difficult circumstances. Sometimes there are private troubles — these are secrets between the Father and His child. Sometimes there is just the pressure of the ordinary, only we seem to feel it more, perhaps because we are tired after going through some spiritual experience which has left the body weary even though the heart is happy. It helps us to remember that every test is a trust. Our Lord trusts us to stand the test by His grace and not to give way. It helps, too, to remember that no test lasts for ever. It is a passing thing.

Hear what comfortable words our Father says to you about your soul which He has redeemed: "I the Lord do keep it; I will water it every moment: lest any hurt it, I will keep it night and day." Isa. 27.3.

Psa. 4.1: *Thou hast enlarged me when I was in distress.*

The more one thinks of these words the more they open their wonderful meaning. Darby renders it, "In pressure, Thou hast enlarged me"; and Kay, "In straits Thou madest wide room for me". Whatever the pressure be, in that pressure — think of it — enlargement; the very opposite of what the word "pressure" suggests; and room, plenty of room, in a strait place.

We may sometimes feel distressed: here then is a word of pure hope and strong consolation. No distress need cramp us, crowd us into ourselves, make us smaller and poorer in anything that matters. Largeness, like the largeness of the sea, is His gift to us. We shall not be flattened in spirit by pressure, but enlarged; in the narrow ways of pain or of temptation He will make wide room for us.

In the last verse but one of 1 John, I found a lovely and, to me, new light on the great story of Job. During his long trial Job said, "Oh that I were as in months past, as in the days when God preserved me; when His candle shined upon my head, and when by His light I walked through darkness".[1] Do we not all but see the Heavenly watchers as they listened and longed (if we may think in such human ways of them) that he might know what they had seen on those two days when Satan came among the sons of God and dared to challenge Him, and God took up the challenge[2] (so brave is the love of God)?

But if Job had known, we should never have had that mighty story, nor would he ever have known his God as he knew Him at the end of that long tyranny. "I have heard of Thee by the hearing of the ear: but now mine eye seeth Thee".[3]

"And we know that the Son of God is come, and hath given us an understanding, that we may know Him that is true".[4] This was my new light on Job. It cost Job what we know, and it cost John what we do not know (Patmos and all that lay behind and that followed after — the long martyrdom of life), to come to understand Him that is true.

In the hour of Job's deepest despondency he wished to be as he was when "the intimacy of God was over [his] tent",[5] and he did not know that, even then, he was very near to a more wonderful intimacy than had ever been his before. Is it not joyful to think that it may be so with us? Today, even today, we may be on the verge of——what?

[1]Job 29.2, 3. [2]Job 1, 2. [3]Job 42.5. [4]1 Jn. 5.20.
[5]Job 29.4, Roth.

Heb. 10.32: *After ye were illuminated, ye endured a great fight of afflictions.*

Have you ever wondered how it is that just after you had been "illuminated" in some way, perhaps specially comforted or strengthened, "a great fight of afflictions" has followed? We are not told why this is so, but the words tell us that we are not the first to experience this test of faith.

This morning these words came to me with piercing power: "That no man should be moved by these afflictions: for yourselves know that we are appointed thereunto."[1] I think that we are often inclined to be surprised when things are difficult or painful. We entirely forget that we "are appointed thereunto." Let us lay hold on those words *appointed thereunto,* and we shall not expect the way of the Cross to be like a lovely forest path.

But remember this: These afflictions, temptations, trials of the flesh or spirit, are not worthy to be compared with what is going to be revealed (it is not revealed yet). Read Romans 8.18, and take courage.

[1]1 Thess. 3.3.

In the wall of the Kremlin (the great fortress of Moscow) there is, or was once, a little church. In that little church a beautiful name was given to the mother of our Lord Jesus Christ. She was called the *Lady of Unexpected Joy*. This name has been much in my mind of late. I had thought of her, rather, as one whose soul was pierced with the sword of suffering, but in her lovely song of thanksgiving she looks on to the joy, and the grace that was given to her then must have been with her to the end. Through pain, in pain, after pain, it was given to her to be the "Lady of Unexpected Joy."

All through the New Testament and in parts of the Old, we see the sword that pierces the soul alongside "an unexpected joy". Our Lord's words in Mark 10.29, 30 put the sword last, perhaps because it is so true that He gives of His Heavenly riches before He asks us to suffer. But however the words are arranged we find them together. The "not only . . . but also" of Philippians 1.29 runs through the gospel; it is never disguised. The rose is set on a thorny stem. This is my word for you today. Is there in any heart something that is like the piercing of a sword? Then watch for the unexpected joy. It will come sooner or later. The rosebud will form and open, and the rose appear. "Though it tarry, wait for it; because it will surely come, it will not tarry." Hab. 2.3.

How beautifully and how surely the word of God finds us just where we are. We prove it again and again. "The Word was made flesh, and dwelt among us"[1] — that explains it. "In that He Himself hath suffered being tempted, He is able to succour them that are tempted."[2]

Today I read what has often cheered me before, but how
much more now. "The word of God is not bound."[3]	It
rings out so triumphantly that it sounds like a song.	What
do bonds matter when that word is true?	Often in our early
days here in India, when houses were closed to us because
of someone confessing Christ, this assurance gave us com-
fort.	It is so now in many lands.	"But there is no prison
for the word of God."[4]	Hearts may close against His loving
influences and we may feel bound and helpless; but the word
of God can penetrate — and just as it does with us, so it
will do with them — it will find them where they are.	I
want to learn to trust more hopefully and joyfully in the
effective, the illuminating and the loving word of God.	*The
word of God is not bound.*	Does this not bring good cheer
to us all?

    [1]Jn. 1.14.   [2]Heb. 2.18.   [3]2 Tim. 2.9.   [4]Moff.

Psa. 48.8, P.B.V.: *We wait for Thy loving-kindness, O
God.*

Wars and rumours of wars are everywhere now, and we
know that dark days are coming on the earth; but through
all the thousand clamours that even now we cannot help
hearing, these calm words come like the sound of bells
through storm: "We wait for Thy loving-kindness, O God,
in the midst of Thy temple."

So within, all is peace.	"All hail [*lit.* rejoice]",[1] said our
Risen Saviour to the troubled women; "Be of good cheer",
"Peace be unto you",[2] He said to His poor fearful disciples.
What is round the next corner?	We do not know; but we
do know that we shall find that of which "we have

thought",[3] that for which we wait — that which we expect — the loving-kindness of our God.

Things were dark in the political world when Elijah said, "It is enough"; but we know what was happening in the spiritual world at that moment — an angel was on his way to succour him.[4]   They were dark when Elisha said, "Why should I wait for the Lord any longer?" but in the spiritual world things were happening, for the Lord made the host of the Syrians to hear a noise of chariots and a noise of horses, even the noise of a great host.[5]

Some of Mr. Churchill's* words are great for our work and warfare: "Let us move forward steadfastly, together, into the storm and through the storm".   "Into . . . through" — yes, that is it.

Be of good courage.   Be of good cheer.

[1]Matt. 28.9.   [2]Jn. 16.33; 20.19.   [3]Psa. 48.9, A.V.
[4]1 Kings 19.4-8.   [5]2 Kings 6.33, R.V.; 7.6.

I have been reading 1 Thessalonians over again today, the first letter of St. Paul's that the Holy Spirit has preserved for us.   I had not noticed before that in this letter for the first time the joy of God the Holy Ghost is mentioned. That joy is bound up with trial for Christ's sake: "Having received the word in much affliction, with joy of the Holy Ghost".[1]

Nothing *we* are called to go through can compare with the terrific trials of those days, and yet we may lose something by forgetting that even in our far lesser experiences we may know this special joy.   And to those who have lately begun their missionary service, the rendings of the first year, the pull of home thoughts and longings, the

*Now Sir Winston Churchill.

struggle through the ineffectiveness of speaking in a new language, the desperate feeling of limitation and the temptation that belongs to that feeling, all these together do make a trial keen enough to require something very special in the way of help. Here it is in this letter:

(1) "You are beloved by God and . . . He has chosen you." Ch. 1.4, Weym.

(2) "None of you should waver in these afflictions; since you know yourselves that such is our appointed lot". Ch. 3.3, Con.

(3) "May God Himself, who gives peace, make you entirely holy; and may your spirits, souls and bodies be preserved complete and be found blameless at the Coming of our Lord Jesus Christ. Faithful is He who calls you, and He will also perfect His work." Ch. 5.23, 24, Weym.

[1]Ch. 1.6.

Acts 10.38: *Jesus of Nazareth . . . went about doing good.*

Heb. 12.2: *Who for the joy that was set before Him endured the cross.*

Matt. 10.24, 25: *The disciple is not above his Master. . . . It is enough for the disciple that he be as his Master.*

There are times in life when the sky is so blue and the air so fresh, and all things so lovely, that when reading such words as these, the disciple who does truly want to follow his Master and be as his Master is almost troubled, wondering whether he is missing something his Master had. But sooner or later, to the willing-hearted the cup is given. It is for the Lord, not the servant, to choose when and how.

And the word, "Who for the joy that was set before Him endured the cross", seems to me to carry triumph. He who endured for the joy that was set before Him, endured with joyfulness. We cannot imagine Him depressed, "under the weather", going about with a look in His face that told everybody how much He was enduring.

We shall never do more than taste the cup He drank to the bitter dregs; but should we ever be inclined to magnify things, and weaken, is it not a comfort to remember that there is One alongside who can in one bright moment give unto us "beauty for ashes, the oil of joy for mourning, the garment of praise for the spirit of heaviness . . . that He might be glorified"? Isa. 61.3.

I have often noticed that just after we have been very much refreshed by some brook in the way, there is dryness, or strong temptation to that dreary thing. It seems strange that it can be so, but it is so.

"Oh that He would give me more than paper-grace and tongue-grace", Samuel Rutherford said nearly 300 years ago, and in the hours before the dawn this morning I said it too. I do so fear sometimes lest these Notes which have slipped into being a custom should be only paper-grace and tongue-grace. Then came dawn and *Daily Light,* and five words seemed to leap from the page, *Even as I also overcame.*[1] Do we not sometimes lose our succour by thinking that our Lord walked triumphantly through life, because, being Divine, He could not do anything else? But these words suggest a real fight, and if "in all points tempted like as we are" is to mean anything to us, we must believe it includes even this that can try us so much. Moreover, He *"suffered* being tempted."

"Even as I also overcame" — the Lord make us His overcomers. "He hath delivered my soul in peace from the battle that was against me".[2] "He hath completely redeemed my soul out of the attack upon me," is Rotherham's rendering of that glorious verse.

[1]Rev. 3.21.   [2]Psa. 55.18.

Is there any grief so sharp, so comfortless, as the grief of seeing the love that won on Calvary wronged and grieved? Sometimes painful things must be done (see, for example, 1 Cor. 5.5; 1 Tim. 1.19, 20). Such hours must sometimes be. Was it because our Lord knew of that painful "must" that He included in the little trusted group of twelve one whom He knew would be disloyal?[1] In our sorrow at such times we turn to the One who understands. He has walked on this same road before, only, as always, so much further on than we are called to go.

Some words from *The Imitation** have often brought me to the place where I would be. It is so fatally easy to forget that we are not here to enjoy life, to live pleasantly, without stabs and rending griefs that leave scars. The first sign showing that we are in danger of forgetting is when we feel surprise at the thrust of the spear.

"Weenest thou to escape what never mortal man might escape? What saint in this world was without cross and tribulation? Not our Lord Jesus Christ was without sorrow of His Passion one hour in all His life. He saith, 'It behoveth Christ to suffer and to rise from death, and so to enter into His glory.' And how seekest thou another way than the King's high way, the Cross way? *All Christ's life was a cross and a martyrdom: and thou seekest to thyself rest and joy?*"

**Of the Imitation of Christ*, by Thomas a Kempis.

The Lord bring us to the place where we shall be surprised not because of battle-wounds, but because of respite from them. "That I may know Him, and the power of His resurrection, and the fellowship of His sufferings"[2] — Lord, bring us, keep us, there.

[1]Jn. 6.64, 70, 71.   [2]Phil. 3.10.

In the Bible we have "the heart of God in the words of God", as someone said hundreds of years ago; and now here is something for you from the heart of God in the words of God:

> *He had in His right hand seven stars.* Rev. 1.16.
> *He laid His right hand upon me, saying unto me, Fear not. v.* 17.

Did you ever fear a little as you thought of the difficulties ahead? Did you ever think, "The Lord Jesus has so many to take care of, how will He have time to think of me"? We have the answer to such thoughts here. It is the Hand that holds the seven stars (the seven churches, all the worlds and the Heaven of heavens), it is *that* Hand that is laid upon each one of us, and to each one the word is the same, "Fear not".

This does not mean that there will not be difficulties and hard fights, and (if we are real soldiers) battle-wounds. Look at the next "Fear not". "Fear none of those things which thou shalt suffer".[1] The Revised Version, keeping closer to the Greek, I suppose, has "Fear not the things which thou art about to suffer". In the day when those words were written, the things that true Christians were about to suffer were terrific. But even though we have not to go through torture of the body, we shall all have to endure something which is really suffering, and which God knows is suffering; and so we have the glorious word at the outset, "Fear none of those things . . .; be thou faithful unto death, and I will give thee a crown of life."

[1]Rev. 2.10.

There are always some who are going through sharp trial, and who will fail unless they remember whom they are following — not a Christ at ease, but the Christ who was crucified.

I am sure, for I have proved it true, that one long look at Calvary does something for us that nothing else can do. *Consider Him that endured . . . lest ye be wearied and faint in your minds.*[1] Try it, you who are in the thick of things. Try it, and you will prove the power that is in it. If there has been defeat anywhere and you are tempted to "faint in your minds", do not be discouraged, but determine that next time attack comes you will win. "Consider Him that endured", and you will be more than conqueror. I am reading Romans 8 over and over just now. This is Way's rendering of *v.* 37: "Amidst all this *we* are the victors — ay, more than victors, in the might of Him who hath loved us!"

I have ceased to ask for easy ways for those I love most dearly. I ask instead for a conquering faith, for strength and the blessing of peace. "The Lord sitteth upon the flood [any flood, every flood]; yea, the Lord sitteth King for ever. The Lord will give strength unto His people; the Lord will bless His people with peace."[2]

[1]Heb. 12.3.   [2]Psa. 29.10, 11.

Days of joyful victory hold their test. Is the soul humble enough to come through unscathed? But there is a terrible power, too, in days when the only word that expresses life is, "And it was given unto him to make war with the saints, *and to overcome them.*"[1]

Some years ago we were caught in the turmoil of Law Court trouble; it lasted for many months, and utterly exhausted those of us who were submerged in it. During that time a friend came for a visit, and his (as it seemed to me) light faith was a trial, not a help. *Of course,* we should win, he said — "Power over all the power of the enemy" — was not that our Lord's own word? What need for anxiety? Everything would be all right. I remember thanking God for the Psalms with their cries from the depths. This shallow sureness got me nowhere. I could not forget "But if not . . ."[2]

I do not think we should ever forget that "must" of our Lord Jesus, spoken just after the shining word about His coming: "So shall also the Son of man be in His day. But first must He suffer many things".[3] They followed a suffering Saviour, the warrior souls and heroes of faith all down the ages, and among them were some who were tortured, not accepting — not able to accept — deliverance.

All through Scripture there is a sense as of tremendous forces held in leash. "Thinkest thou that I cannot now pray to My Father, and He shall presently give Me more than twelve legions of angels? But how then shall the Scriptures be fulfilled, that thus it must be?"[4]

There is darkness set in the heart of the ways of God, a darkness of which all know something, except those who only play round the edges of these matters. It is dark as we penetrate further in, but that darkness will one day pass into the glory of the city whose light is like unto a stone

most precious.[5]   I have found my comfort in these words,
"Here is an opportunity for endurance, and for the exercise
of faith, on the part of God's people"[6] — and this opportunity will never come again.

[1]Rev. 13.7.   [2]Dan. 3.17, 18.   [3]Luke 17.24, 25.
[4]Matt. 26.53, 54.   [5]Rev. 21.11.   [6]Rev. 13.10, Weym.

2 Cor. 4.8, 9, Way:

> *On every hand hard-pressed . . . yet not crushed.*
> *In desperate plight . . . yet not in despair.*
> *Close followed by pursuers — yet not abandoned.*
> *Beaten to the earth — yet never destroyed.*

I have often seen St. Paul in these words; but today,
thinking over our Lord's last days of earthly life, it seemed
to me that, as His true follower wrote the words, he must
have seen his Master on the road before him.   "In many-
sided endurance — amid afflictions, sore straits, and priva-
tions, amid scourgings, prison-cells, and riots, amid toils,
night-vigils, and fastings — purity, in spiritual illumination,
in long-suffering, in kindness, in the Holy Spirit's presence,
in love unfeigned,"[1] — how such words show Him; how
they shame us.   What do we know of any of these things?
What do I know?

It was a day when the thought of this was vivid that these
words came:

> No wound?   No scar?
> Yet as the Master shall the servant be,
> And piercèd are the feet that follow Me;
> But thine are whole: can he have followed far
> Who has nor wound, nor scar?

If ever the pin-pricks of life try to show themselves as sword-wounds, and the sorrows of life try to darken our sky, and we are tempted to make the worst of anything — perhaps even some small thing that following the Crucified costs us — oh, let us look at His scars.

[1]2 Cor. 6.4-6, Way.

CHAPTER 7

"THAT WE . . . MAY GROW UP INTO HIM IN ALL THINGS"

Ephesians 4.14, 15

Gal. 5.22, Weym: *The Spirit . . . brings a harvest of love, joy, peace, patience towards others . . . .*

Moffatt translates "patience" by *good temper*. Both words will help us. Is it not a comfort to remember that God knows we need such ordinary commonplace blessings as good temper? And is it not a strength to remember, when we feel our patience wearing thin, that "patience towards others" is a gift to be had? We can easily get to the end of our own sweetness of spirit, but not to the end of our God's.

Let us reap in this harvest field.

Good Manners

One of my dearest friends wrote these words in a beautiful poem called *Prayer before Nature*:

"Anoint mine eyes with eye-salve, mighty Saviour,
　　As through this wonder-world of Thine I stray,
Let nought in my soul's gesture or behaviour
　　Obstruct sweet glimpses of Thyself today."

If we pray that prayer truly, we shall not, by little acts of careless rudeness, make it harder for others to see the Lord Jesus.   And if anyone is inclined to think that rudeness and honesty run together, and politeness and insincerity, I will tell you what I have found: The strongest, bravest, truest people I ever knew were (are) the most gentle-mannered. Good manners are not among the things that do not matter. Can we imagine our Lord Jesus ever being rude?

Psa. 119.65, 66, LXX: *Thou hast wrought kindly with Thy servant, O Lord. . . . Teach me kindness.*

I do not find this translation anywhere but in the Septuagint, and yet as it is there I give it to you with confidence. The glorious Sun has shone upon us.   It did not scorch us, as it might have done, sinners of earth as we are; it bathed us in brightness.   "Thou hast wrought kindly with Thy servant, O Lord. . . . Teach me kindness".   "Who is as the Lord our God?   Who dwells in the high places, and yet looks upon the low things in Heaven, and on the earth"[1] — are we not the low things on the earth?

Love looks upon the low things, Love is kind to common things, for Love loves the unlovable.   Thus hast Thou loved me, O Lord.   Thou hast wrought kindly with me indeed. "Teach me kindness".

In one of John Buchan's books, which are almost always far more than mere stories, I found this beautiful sentence, "Had ever anyone made so much music in the world by merely passing through it?"   And someone else has written, speaking of one who lived this life, "She doeth little kindnesses that most leave undone or despise."   I think there is a great deal in the words, "that most leave undone".   Per-

haps they think them too small to do.   But is anything
small that helps to make another happy?   The Second Mile
has been described as "the loving little extra things that
need not be done, but which Love loves to do just because
it loves."

So, Lord, "teach me kindness", and enable me to live
this life.

¹Psa. 113.5, 6, LXX.

A day or two ago one who was with me prayed like this,
"Lord, help me to welcome interruptions, especially when
the interruption seems less important than the work I am
trying to do."   That prayer has often been mine.   I expect
many of you have felt the need of the loving grace of the
Lord to help you to welcome interruptions, especially when
they do not seem to matter nearly so much as what we are
doing at the moment.   Thinking of this, I found myself this
early morning in Luke 9.11, R.V.   The people followed our
Lord Jesus (He had wanted to be alone with His disciples
just then), *and He welcomed them.*

It is so easy to be too preoccupied to be welcoming.   May
the love of our Lord Jesus, for whose sake and in whose
service we are here, so overflow from us that it will be
natural for us to do as He would and be welcoming.

Comfort

Many think of comfort as if it were a gentle kind of
soothing and nothing else.   But the Oxford Dictionary gives
its derivation, *con fortare.*   So "to strengthen" is its first

meaning.   And it has been explained beautifully, I think, as "to raise up from depression."

I have heard one who was, as she thought, comforting another, say, "How hard it is for you"; but that sort of talk does not raise up, it pushes down.   It is weakening, not strengthening.   God's comfort is never weakening; He leaves the soul He comforts stronger to fight, braver to suffer, grateful, not sorry for itself, keen to go on "to strive, to seek, to find, and not to yield."

At the completion of the reading of any of the books of Moses in the synagogue, it was the custom for the congregation to exclaim, "Be strong, be strong, and let us strengthen one another!"   In like manner, when we see others under the enemy's attack, let us brace and strengthen them.

God make us all comforters in that strong sense of the word — His fellow-comforters.

Someone has said,

"What we can suffer for another is the test of love;
    What we can do for another is the test of power";

and the following lines carry on the thought:

"God — let me be aware,
    Stab my soul fiercely with another's pain;
    Let me walk, seeing horror and stain;
    Let my hands, groping, find other hands.
    Give me the heart that divines and understands —
    Give me the courage, wounded, to fight;
    Flood me with knowledge, drench me with light."*

*From a Californian magazine called *Light*.

Eph. 3.19: *To know the love of Christ, which passeth knowledge, that ye might be filled with all the fulness of God.*

I am sure that some among us are longing to know more of the blessed love of God, longing to love with His love, to live the life that is love through and through. I do not think that such a desire is ever created in the heart unless there is going to be a fulfilment. "Blessed are they which do hunger and thirst . . . [after love]: for they shall be filled."

There is only one thing that can hinder the love of God from flowing into our hearts. Take the Forest Pool as an illustration. If the catchment area up in the mountains is full to overflowing, what can hinder the flow down to the Pool? Only one thing — a blocked channel. I wonder if you will all see the hope and the comfort that there is in this. It means that the moment the hindrance to love is removed (washed away by the forces of Love itself) that moment the waters of love will flow. It must be so. It cannot be otherwise. Pray in faith, then, today; direct your prayer to the revealing and removing of the hindrance. Love, eternal Love, will do the rest.

John 1.16: *And of his fulness have all we received, and grace for grace.*

Is it not good that this means we have received grace after grace from His fulness, grace upon grace? More and more the love of God seems to me like the sea. There is no end to the grace of love, for there is no end to the ocean of love, and to be "filled with all the fulness of God" must mean just to sink like a shell into that sea, till all that is not love is washed out, and there is nothing but love.

> As empty shell in depths of sea,
> So would I sink, be filled with Thee.

Does anyone feel discouraged today, at the end of love and the patience of love? Do not be discouraged. Dip your shell into that sea. Sink down into that sea. Let it fill you. Love full fills. The grace of love flows from a fulness that cannot run dry. To Him who is Love be glory.

Worm and pearl

Some years ago a fleet of pearlers fished for pearls in the sea off Bathurst Island. Sometimes hundreds of oysters are brought up by the divers before they find a pearl of any value. When they find a big pearl there is great excitement and joy. One day, a diver in that fleet found an oyster with a pearl as large as a pigeon's egg in it. Such a pearl would be worth about £20,000; but when the diver gave that oyster to the delighted owner of the fleet, and he began to clean the outside of the shell before chipping out the pearl, he found that a marine worm had bored a hole from the outside through the shell and into the heart of the pearl; and so it was not worth anything at all. A ruined pearl is worthless. The ruin was wrought by a single tiny worm. This story will speak to every one of us if we give it time. It needs no explanation. It explains itself. May God give it to us to fear sin and save us from saying, "It is only a little sin." That worm was only a little worm, but——

The oyster could not prevent the worm from boring a

hole in its shell. We can. The moment we feel a worm crawling on our shell we can get rid of it. We cannot prevent it from choosing our shell as a nice place to crawl upon, but we can make sure that it will be swept off the moment we know it is there. Is this not a comfort?

I have been much helped of late by Isaiah 59.18, 19. I found in the Revised Version and other versions that the thought is not of the enemy coming in like a flood, but of the Lord Himself as a rushing stream which causes His enemies to fear; for He comes as "fury to His adversaries." To keep to the illustration, it is as though we saw His glorious might sweeping the worm off — how could it stand against a flood that "the breath of the Lord driveth"?

So there is nothing to fear. If we keep ourselves in the love of God — and we can if we will — then that mighty stream of Love, driven by the breath of the Lord, will so flow over us that no worm shall have a chance to burrow in and spoil our pearl.

In case any are puzzled by these two different translations of Isaiah 59.19, I suggest this way out of the puzzle: Take both. In that particular verse, though some versions understand the meaning to be what I wrote, the Revised Version margin has, "*Or,* When the adversary shall come in like a flood, the Spirit of the Lord shall lift up a standard against him." So there was a doubt in the minds of the translators, though they leaned to the meaning they gave in the text. When that is so I think we are allowed to take all the wealth of strength and comfort that is to be found in both. When both meanings are true to a spiritual fact, we may, I think, trust to the Eternal Spirit, the Writer of the words, to open them to us in the way that will most perfectly meet our needs.

Do I feel very much like an oyster with a worm crawling

on its shell? Then thank God for the mighty "rushing stream, which the breath of the Lord driveth." No worm that ever was or shall be can stand against that. Am I a soldier out on the field, and does the enemy come in like a flood, many and many a time? Then thank God for the blessed Spirit of God who lifts up a standard against him. Either way it is "fury to His adversaries", and my adversaries are His. Let us trust and not be afraid, and give thanks unto His Name.

I have lately found these words written by Caroline Fry:

"Humility, the fairest, loveliest flower
That bloomed in Paradise; the first that died—
It is so frail and delicate a thing
That if it look upon itself 'tis gone;
And he who ventures to esteem it his,
Shows by that very thought he has it not."

Have you ever humbly prayed this prayer, "Lord Jesus, show me myself as Thou dost see me"? The other half of that prayer is, "Show me Thyself." "Show me myself, that I may fall in the dust before Thee. Show me Thyself, that I may see the love that redeemed me and strengthens me to serve in joyful gratitude."

While I was reading Conybeare's translation of St. Paul's letters to his dear converts, the thought came that one way by which we can see our Lord Jesus is to look at the love that He puts into the hearts of His servants. How tenderly

Paul loved; how earnestly he longed; how tenderly he wrote (how bravely, too; he never wrote smooth things); how utterly his life was bound up with those whom he loved: "I live, if you be steadfast in the Lord." 1 Thess. 3.8, Con.

Dr. Way has a lovely thought in his free rendering of Philippians 4.10. He understands the words translated "in the Lord" to suggest *the nearness of the Lord.* So the loving gift of the Philippians made St. Paul feel the nearness of his Lord so much that he rejoiced greatly. I have often wondered why it is that some little act does one good and makes one glad far out of proportion to its apparent importance. The mere coming into the room of one who is loving, the least touch or glance or word (or, often, presence without a word) rests and comforts and refreshes. I have felt it was the flowing out of that most Heavenly thing, love, that did it; but this thought goes behind that and explains it. "It made me feel the nearness of the Lord". Is it not beautiful and joyful to know that everything that happens is bound by invisible cords to the spiritual world and to Him who rules there and is our Beloved?

Hebrews 5.12-14 is much in my mind. I sometimes hear people murmur about being only babes in Christ, and it sounds beautifully humble. But is it? Should we like our babies to go on babyishly? Is it not rather that we have stuck somewhere, turned aside from, slipped from under, some word of the Lord that required self-discipline in an ignoring of likes and dislikes, and so have failed to grow up? "Each age has its proper food," Westcott says about these verses, "but spiritual maturity comes through discipline and not through years only." Here the "discernment of good and evil" is regarded in relation to the proper food of the soul, the discrimination of that which contributes to its due strengthening.

What food is strong meat? I think two words of our Lord, one to Satan, the other to His disciples, give the perfect answer. "Man shall . . . live . . . by every word that proceedeth out of the mouth of God"[1] — every word — not only the comfortable words. "I have meat to eat that ye know not of. . . . My meat is to do the will of Him that sent Me, and to finish His work."[2] Part of the will and the work was (according to Psalm 40.10 and many similar words) the *not* hiding, the *not* concealing, but the lavish giving of love, as here by the well of Samaria.

Is it not possible that some among us are babes still, satisfied with "milk" (that is to say, the part of the revelation of God which appears to make little demand upon us), and that we have never wholeheartedly gone on to take the food that is meant for us, the strong meat that our Lord and His warriors all down the ages lived upon; and for that reason we have failed to grow up?

May the Lord help us to smash our baby-bottles and teach us how to feed on His strong meat.

[1]Matt. 4.4.   [2]John 4.32, 34.

I read one day of an electric appliance by which the hulls of vessels could be kept clear of the barnacles, sea-weeds, and other growths which would lessen their speed and hinder progress. It used to be necessary to take a ship into dock to remove these hindrances. When I read that they are now able to keep a ship's hull clear by this new invention, I said, "Lord, Thou wilt — yea, Thou dost —

keep my unseen life, my life 'below the watch-line', clear
and detached. Thou wilt not let me get slower in spirit as
I near the harbour."

Each day brings us a day nearer the end of our journey.
The Lord keep our hulls clear, that we do not get slower in
spirit as we near the harbour.

Prov. 27.21, R.V.: *A man is tried by his praise.*

Will you ponder that word? How does praise affect you?
Are you uplifted by it, or are you humbled? Do you feel,
"I really must be rather a special person", or do you feel,
"How little the one who speaks like that knows me"? Does
praise make you careless about your work, or far more
careful? Do you take it to yourself, or lay it at His feet to
whom alone any good in you is due? for what have we that
we have not received? Those and many other questions
will come to your heart as you think over these words.
When God allows you to be tried by praise, what comes
out of that crucible — gold, or dross?

If a man is tried by the way he bears praise, I think he is
equally tried by the way he takes blame. The head of a
college said to a friend of mine, "When I have to speak
to anyone about something wrong and the first reaction is,
'I wonder who told that of me', then my heart sinks." I
well understood that feeling. When someone tells us of
something wrong in us, how do we take it? Do we wonder
who told that of us? Do we make excuses? Do we blame
somebody else, or circumstances? Do we say like Saul, "I
have sinned: yet honour me now, I pray thee, before the
elders of my people, and before Israel";[1] in other words,

"I hope nobody else need know"? Or do we say like David, "Against Thee, Thee only, have I sinned, and done this evil in Thy sight"?[2]

[1]1 Sam. 15.30.   [2]Psa. 51.4.

Numbers 32.

When the children of Reuben and the children of Gad wanted the land of Gilead because it was a good place for their cattle, we do not know whether they meant to do the selfish thing which Moses took for granted was in their minds: "Shall your brethren go to war, and shall ye sit here?"[1] Perhaps they did not really mean to do that. Perhaps they did, and now saw themselves as cravens and were ashamed. What strikes me as important in the story is in the words, "And they came near unto him".[2] Moses had spoken exceedingly straight. They were not huffy. *They came near unto him.*

If we are misunderstood, or if quite justly some hidden selfishness is exposed, what is the first reaction of the natural man towards the one who misunderstands, or who uncovers selfishness? Is it not to go away and nurse the grievance? But these men did not do that. They *came near* unto Moses, and all was cleared up, and all went well.

[1]*v.* 6.   [2]*v.* 16.

John 8.54, R.V.: *If I glorify Myself, My glory is nothing.*

This word strikes deep. It cuts straight through all self-praise, all pleasure in praise, all taking home to one's heart what others say.

It seems to me to be like a hand dashing the cup of praise — or that subtle thing, spiritual flattery — from our lips. I believe that the only safe place for praise of any sort is in the dust at the foot of the Cross. I am not thinking now of the encouraging word that a captain speaks to his soldiers, or a fellow-worker to fellow-workers, or a teacher to children. I am thinking of that deadly thing, the praise of man that bringeth a snare, not a blessing. It is the acceptance of *that* which wrecks the soul. Our Lord utterly refused it, ignored it, turned from it. It was nothing, less than nothing, to Him.

"And every one be tender of the Glory of God, and be careful that in no ways His Name and truth be dishonoured." This is from a letter which George Fox wrote in 1667. I think you will feel, as I did when I read it, that you want to remember those words. Think of the eye, its preciousness, our care of it, and what it means to hurt it, as an illustration. Be tender of the glory of God as you would be tender of the apple of your eye (the "jewel of the eye" as it is in Tamil). Our God uses this same illustration for tenderness: "He kept him as the apple of His eye";[1] "He that toucheth you toucheth the apple of His eye";[2] and we have the prayer, "Keep me as the apple of the eye";[3] and once the word is used in a way that connects with George Fox's thought, "Keep . . . My law as the apple of thine eye."[4] The law of God is the law of love. To keep it in sincerity always leads to a great tenderness of spirit where the glory of the Lord is concerned. Be very careful to keep the law of love, lest in anything your God be dishonoured; and as you would be tender of the most precious possession you have, even so "be tender of the Glory of God".

Lord Jesus, for me crucified,
Let not my footsteps from Thee slide,
For I would tread where Thou hast trod,
My spirit tender of the Glory of God.

That Glory which meant all to Thee,
Let it mean all, my Lord, to me;
So would I tread where Thou hast trod,
My spirit tender of the Glory of God.

[1]Deut. 32.10.   [2]Zech. 2.8.   [3]Psa. 17.8.   [4]Prov. 7.2.

Going through the mill

2 Cor. 1.8: *Pressed out of measure, above strength.*
Exceedingly beyond power were we weighed down.
(Roth.)
Crushed, crushed far more than I could stand. (Moff.)
Exceedingly weighed down, and felt overwhelmed.
(Weym.)

This is what we mean by going "through the mill". But would any one of us wish to escape this pressure? We can if we choose. It is possible to pass through life without knowing much of what Paul wrote of as an ordinary experience. But if we are in earnest to know our Lord, "the power of His resurrection, and the fellowship of His sufferings,"[1] then we shall be crushed and ground between the upper and nether millstones, we shall often be pressed out of measure, above strength, weighed down exceedingly beyond our power, crushed far more than we can stand; being weighed down we shall feel overwhelmed. And yet we shall *not* be overwhelmed. Paul was not. All that we mean by "the mill" will turn to eternal good, and (I think this is the gladdest good of all) will make us more able to help others. So, do not let us be surprised as though some strange thing happened unto us when we feel the feelings of 2 Corinthians 1.8. A minute or two before those words were written, Paul wrote verses 3 and 4: "Blessed be God, even the Father of our Lord Jesus Christ, the Father of mercies, and the God of all comfort; who comforteth us in all our tribulation, that we may be able to comfort them which are in any trouble, by the comfort wherewith we ourselves are comforted of God."

[1]Phil. 3.10.

Fine Flour

When I was small I used to thrust my hands into the flour-bin, whenever I had the chance; not sealskin, kitten's fur or velvet, or even water, seemed to me as wonderful in deliciousness of gentleness as that fine flour.

Later when I read Leviticus and Numbers, and found fine flour was used as a type of our Lord Jesus Christ, I understood at least one reason why He who was the strongest, the bravest, He who set His face as a flint, was, in the texture of His being, as fine flour. Fine flour is flour which has been milled to the uttermost. The natural man abominates the mill. Our holy Saviour was fine flour from the beginning, and yet in an awful sense, He "went through the mill" of hard human experience: He suffered, being tempted; He was crushed (Young gives the word "crushed" in translating "fine" flour).

I have been reading about friction. The microscope shows the surface of, for example, wood, even planed wood, to be covered with what look like prickles. Two surfaces meet, there is friction. Friction is caused by the presence of prickles. To each Christian soul there comes the choice: Will you at all costs be made as fine flour, or are you content to be covered with prickles to the end? It is self in one form or another that makes us prickly. We come up against difficult things, or people, and there is friction of the spirit. It was not so with our dear Lord. "The meekness and gentleness of Christ,"[1] the yieldingness, the self-forgetfulness, show the fine flour in a very lovely way — the sweetness of His nature could not be ruffled. So let us never try to slip out from between the millstones. Let us trust and not be afraid.

As we think of how very unlike fine flour we are, these words come as strong consolation: "The Lord will perfect that which concerneth me".[2] "The disciple is not above his Master: but everyone shall be perfected as his Master."[3] "It doth not yet appear what we shall be: but we know that, when He shall appear, we shall be like Him; for we shall see Him as He is."[4]

[1]2 Cor. 10.1.   [2]Psa. 138.8.   [3]Luke 6.40, mar.   [4]1 John 3.2.

The Bible is full of great words for God's warriors. They sound like trumpets. But there are other words that speak very quietly deep within us. Perhaps there are some who are sorely tempted because of the hardness of the work entrusted to them. That which they had hoped for has not happened. Perhaps they feel they cannot go on. At such times, listen, and you will hear the quiet words I spoke of deep within you. They speak of brokenness, "Blow ye the trumpets . . . : and they blew the trumpets, and brake the pitchers".[1] "An alabaster box of ointment . . . very precious; and she brake the box".[2] Jesus "took . . . and . . . blessed, and brake, and gave".[3] "My body, which is broken for you".[4]

> Broken pitchers — and the light shone out.
> Broken box — and the ointment was poured forth.
> Broken bread — and the hungry were fed.
> A broken Body — and the world was redeemed.
>
> As Thou wast broken, O my Lord, for me,
> Let me be broken, Lord, for love of Thee.

[1]Judges 7.18, 19.   [2]Mark 14.3.   [3]Matt. 14.19.   [4]1 Cor. 11.24.

CHAPTER 8

"TEACH ME TO DO THY WILL"

Psalm 143.10

NEARLY 400 years ago Vaughan wrote:

> "I would I were some bird or star
> Fluttering in woods or lifted far
>   Above this inn
>   And road of sin.
> Then either star or bird should be
> Shining or singing still to Thee."

But he had to live the common life in a difficult world, and so have we. I have often noticed that just when we feel most like saying, "I would I were", our God, the God of the spirits of all flesh, meets us with some plain command which pulls us up sharply, and makes us face this eternal truth: *We are not here to wish to be somewhere or something we are not, but to do the thing that pleases Him exactly where we are, and as we are.*

So our "I would I were" becomes *Cause me to hear . . .; cause me to know . . .; teach me to do Thy will.*[1] And should the heart within us fear as we face that way again, instantly the blessed word revives us, "Fear thou not; for I am with thee".[2] "It is God which worketh in you both to will *and to do* of His good pleasure."[3]

[1]Psa. 143.8, 10.   [2]Isa. 41.10.   [3]Phil. 2.13.

John 12.50: *And I know that His commandment is life everlasting.*

"His commandment" means His will made known to His servant. That will, made known, helps us to live; it is life. We all know the words, "In His will is our peace"; here is another saying equally true, *In doing His will is our life.* But it is one thing to agree with this, and perhaps write it in a notebook and quote it in a letter; it is quite another thing faithfully, peacefully, joyfully, to turn it to effect as our Lord Jesus Christ did, day after day. So for today, may He give each of us grace to live as one should who knows that "His commandment is life everlasting."

"The problem of speeding up the movement of a vehicle is that of applying power to overcome friction." This is a quotation from a book called *Quest of Speed.* What hinders our spiritual speed? If there be anything in which my will is not in accord with God's will, then there is friction, and that keeps me back. I cannot fly in spirit ("mount up with wings as eagles"), I cannot "run, and not be weary", I cannot "walk, and not faint", till my will is content with God's will. As I thought over this, I knew that the only way to end the friction is the way shown in that wonderful verse in Isaiah 40.31: "But they that wait upon the Lord shall renew their strength; they shall mount up with wings as eagles; they shall run, and not be weary; and they shall walk, and not faint." "Wait" means *expect, look for, hope.* God has something much better for us than the thing we naturally desire. As we wait with all the desire of our mind fixed on Him, the thing we naturally long for becomes less pressing, the friction ceases, and so we are set free to go on.

God knows there are few things more difficult to do than to give up our own desires. It is not a thing we do once for all, it comes again and again as Satan tries to make friction between our will and God's. Our dear Lord knew this trial of spirit and He gloriously conquered. He can make it possible for us to do what He Himself did in the Garden of Gethsemane. *"My* grace [the grace that was His then] is sufficient for thee".

It helps often, when we feel things most impossibly difficult, to turn from everything and just look at Him. As we look at Him we love Him. We cannot help loving Him, and where love is, there friction is not.

There was a princess of olden times called Catherine. She became a lover of our Lord Jesus Christ. The Roman Emperor Maximian wanted to save her from flames and to raise her to great honour. She could not be moved. She spoke of her Lord: "He is my love, my glory and all my delight."

If any of us are having trial of any sort just now, let us take those glowing words, and say them to our Lord: *Thou art my love, my glory and all my delight.* If we do that, I think somehow, the trial will lose its power.

Psa. 40.10, P.B.V.: *In the volume of the book it is written of me, that I should fulfil Thy will, O my God: I am content to do it.*

I had read through this Psalm when the feeling came that I had missed something — the golden word for myself for the day. I soon found it. All the other versions have the thought of delight in doing His will, but this dear little word *content* is often just the perfect word. Whatever the day's work be, "I am content to do it"; wherever there is something to do which the heart would not naturally choose, "I am content to do it".

2 Cor. 12.10: *Therefore I take pleasure in infirmities, in reproaches, in necessities, in persecutions, in distresses for Christ's sake: for when I am weak, then am I strong.*

I had been thinking in the night of the way our faithful God brings us straight up to a thing we had thought impossible and says, Now do that. And I wondered what "take pleasure" could truly mean, for obviously it must mean something that did not lie on the surface. It did not mean ordinary pleasure. So this morning I looked it up. May it be the light to some of you that it has been to me. "Take pleasure" means "think well". Way has "I am contented", and Moffatt, "satisfied".

Let us bring it to the test of today: Here is something appointed — perhaps the necessity to bear up under an inner weariness (see that simple little word set in the midst of such tremendous things as stripes, imprisonments and perils in 2 Cor. 11.24-28), or the crush and crowd of life with its burden and its heat, and the care that cometh daily, those "watchings often" with God for souls — necessities, all of them, and sometimes very painful.

But the choice comes with each. How shall I meet it? Thinking ill of it? spending ineffective energy in trying to avoid it? or "thinking well" of it, as one of the "all things" of Romans 8.28, and so "content", "satisfied"?

Rom. 12.2: *That good, and acceptable, and perfect, will of God.*

"Acceptable" in Tamil means *lovable, beloved*: and in the preceding verbs I found something strengthening and comforting: "Be ye transformed by the renewing of your mind". It would fare ill with us if He tired of renewing that which does so often faint and fail; for though we do truly choose to prove that good, acceptable, perfect will, and declare it to be beloved, yet sometimes we slip just there, and then comes discouragement. Here is the word for such an hour. We have a God who renews, renews day by day. (The same verb is used in 2 Cor. 4.16: "The inward man is renewed day by day.") *Renewed* in the spirit of our minds — *renewed* in the inward man, not once a year or at some special meeting, but day by day — we can conquer, we can rejoice in the will of God, and we can find it so lovable that we shall never for one moment want anything else.

Rom. 15.3, Way: *Even Messiah never once consulted His own pleasure.*

Our Lord Jesus never once turned to His own desires and took counsel with them as to His actions, never once took into consideration His own feelings or interests.

This is the kind of life to which we have been called. Does it sound impossible? "You have not to do it in your unaided strength: it is God who is all the while supplying the impulse, giving you the power to resolve, the strength to perform, the execution of His good-pleasure."[1]

Do I *will* to do the will of God?   Then God will reinforce
my will and enable me to *do*.   Do I *will* to know the will
of God?   Then I will not take into consideration my own
feelings and interests, "for even Christ pleased not Himself"
— "never once consulted His own pleasure."

There are times when we wish that an angel from Heaven
would come and tell us what we ought to do.   That angel
will not come, but there are guiding lights in the Book that
God has given us, and if only we are honestly willing to
follow those lights, I believe that we do come to know what
we should do.

Am I in perplexity, not knowing which of two paths is
the one for me?   Christ our Lord "never once consulted
His own pleasure."   Is my pleasure coming into the picture?
Am I taking into consideration my own feelings and interests?   Do these come first, and the good of others and the
peaceful conduct of the work committed to me come
second?   Then I may know without a doubt that I am out
of the will of God.   This way will not lead me to where I
shall have most power to help others.   It will lead me into
by-ways.   In that case, if I am in earnest, I will look to
Him, my Lord and Saviour, instantly, for strength to follow
the other path — "for even Messiah never once consulted
His own pleasure."

Another guiding light is the presence of the peace of God.
The absence of that peace is a sign of danger.   So far as I
know, this is something we can count upon for help in dis-
tinguishing between the path of the will of God and the
path of our own will.   I have never known this test to fail.
Sometimes there is pain, personal pain.   Christ is not concerned to make things easy for us.   But peace is the certain
portion of the child of God who is in the will of God.

[1]Phil. 2.13, Way.

When we prepare to do something which we think is the will of our God and then are hindered, how are we to know whether it is that the Spirit suffers us not, or that Satan hinders? I have often been asked this question.

Always at such times I seem to see a glary white road, a broken-down bullock-cart, and two or three tired, hot people under a tree by the roadside (for, mercifully, there was a tree, more or less shady, nearby). We were on our way to a place on the eastern side of the district. Was the Spirit stopping us, or was it Satan? We simply did not know. After a long wait, the bullock-cart wheel was mended, and we took this to mean that Satan had been the hinderer, and went on. We reached the town about moonrise, and sitting in the moonlight near some shining coconut palms, I found a woman who had been longing to hear of our Lord Jesus. She had a heart prepared, and I believe that she believed. Satan cannot hinder us if God means us to go on. That was the lesson I learned that day.

When it is Satan who is hindering, there is always a way round. *I* may be held up, but somebody else will do what I long to do and cannot. This is what happened when Paul could not go to Thessalonica. He seemed to be sorely needed there, for the converts were being persecuted, and his heart was with them. It was only his body that was in Athens just then, and he tried "earnestly, with intense longing" to go to them. "I Paul wanted again and again to do so — but Satan hindered us."[1] So Paul sought for a way round. He could not break through the hindrances which he must have recognized as allowed by his God (otherwise Satan would have had no power at all). He did not fume and worry; he did not waste time and spiritual energy over the problem of permitted hindrances. He sent Timothy[2] (who apparently was not hindered), and Timothy, his "own son in the faith",[3] his "dearly-loved child",[4] did all that was needed. So there was no loss, but rather gain, for if he could have gone himself, the beautiful letter, which has helped so many all down the ages, would probably never have been written. So even though Satan is the visible hinderer, there is nothing to fear, for if we are in the hand of our God then our times are also in His hand, and He turns what seems like loss to gain.

In Acts 16.6-12, the Spirit is the Hinderer. Paul and his companions seem to have recognized this and peacefully turned westward, instead of going to the north, as they had meant to go. We know that they must have been peaceful, because dreams that are really visions do not come to restless souls any more than reflections are seen in restless waters. As soon as the wishes of God were made clear, Paul and his friends found the way was clear to obey — a ship ready to sail to Europe, room in her for passengers, a straight course, all was straightforward now. I have often wondered exactly how they knew who was hindering, but the only answer I have found to that question is in this word of our Lord Jesus: "When He putteth forth His own sheep, He goeth before them, and the sheep follow Him: for they know His voice . . . they know not the voice of strangers. . . . My sheep hear My voice, and I know them, and they follow Me".[5]

It seems clear from what is written in Acts and elsewhere, that if only we refuse to let ourselves be hustled into action before we know what we are meant to do, we shall be given light before we must act. Then all things will fall into line; the practical help required will be given (like the ship waiting at Troas), and our God will command our strength.

[1]1 Thess. 2.17, 18, Weym. [2]1 Thess. 3.1, 2. [3]1 Tim. 1.2.
[4]2 Tim. 1.2, Weym. [5]John 10.4, 5, 27.

Exod. 33.13, 14: *Shew me now Thy way, that I may know
Thee . . . My Presence shall go with thee, and I will
give thee rest.*

This is the perfect word for the new journey of today.
Tonight we shall be a milestone nearer the place where the
traveller stands, when

> . . . o'er the desert's quivering lines
> He sees the City from afar;
> By day a polished pearl it shines,
> By night it glitters like a star."

What irredeemable loss to lose one day by walking
through its hours without being shown the way, that we
may know Him; to be so fussed by the little roughnesses of
the road, that we cannot serve Him with a quiet mind; to
be so ruffled by the gusty winds that we cannot behold as
in a glass the glory of the Lord; that would be eternal loss.
I think it must be our consciousness of the possibility of
this that makes these words what they are to us. We read
them again and again, and drink new courage and comfort
from their deep wells: "My Presence shall go with thee" —
even with thee, weak as thou art in thyself, disappointing
as thou art to thyself and to others — "and I will give
thee rest."

Gen. 5.22, 24: *And Enoch walked with God.*
Gen. 6.9: *And Noah walked with God.*

We read of a word spoken to Noah which revealed that
which was to be, and directed his steps. We do not read of

any such revelation to Enoch; but he walked all day long with his God. The word means *habitually walked* — walked to and fro, and up and down — just the ordinary walk of the ordinary day. His eyes saw the little signs of direction that careless eyes would have missed; he was so much with his God that he learned to know His wishes, and loving Him, pleased Him, satisfied Him,[1] satisfied His heart.

How joyful, how beautiful, it would be if this day, this week, and on till the walk ends, we walked like that. Sometimes, if it be necessary for the fulfilment of His purpose, our God will speak as to Noah (so at least I believe), and then John 10.4, 5 holds the soul in stillness, and so does Exodus 23.21, "Be careful in His presence";[2] but the usual way, it seems to me, is what I think of as the Enoch way. This is the way of Psalm 32.8: "I will guide thee with Mine eye", and many other passages; and our response is Psalm 123.2: "Our eyes wait upon the Lord our God". We find both ways in the Bible, and both in life, and I think we need more and more to ask to be observant, sensitive, towards the "little signs" which, put together where the light of the Scriptures can fall on them, point us right.

So we come back to the old prayer, "Cause me to hear . . .; cause me to know . . .; teach me to do Thy will"; and, lest ear or eye or heart grow dull, let us continually say, "Quicken me, O Lord, for Thy Name's sake".[3]

[1]Heb. 11.5, Way. [2]Darby. [3]Psa. 143.8, 10, 11.

Most of us know the temptation to pray for an interval without that spiritual bearing of burdens that seems to be part of our life. We long for a breathing-space, when — to change the figure — we could lie back on our oars and glide downstream for a while. That time never comes. "A body hast Thou prepared me . . . *to do Thy will, O God*."[1] To do that will must lead us to share in the fellowship of the sufferings of our Lord for the sinful and the weak. And there is no ease in that life.

But there is something better than ease: "The beloved of the Lord shall dwell in safety by Him; and the Lord shall cover him all the day long, and he shall dwell between His shoulders."[2] It is the Shepherd-thought again. But now it is not the lost sheep that is borne, it is the under-shepherd. Burden and all, he is lifted up and borne, so that though there may be what St. Paul called "great heaviness and continual sorrow",[3] yet there is peace — peace unbroken by untoward events, unsurprised when new burdens are added; peace restful, patient, tranquil; peace which accepts all that is allowed to come as within the will of God.

"A body hast Thou prepared me. . . . Lo, *I come* . . . *to do Thy will, O God*."

"Now the God of peace, that brought again from the dead our Lord Jesus, that great Shepherd of the sheep, through the blood of the everlasting covenant, make you perfect in every good work *to do His will,* working in you that which is wellpleasing in His sight, through Jesus Christ; to whom be glory for ever and ever. Amen."[4]

[1]Heb. 10.5, 7. [2]Deut. 33.12. [3]Rom. 9.2. [4]Heb. 13.20, 21.

CHAPTER 9

"ACCEPTABLE SERVICE"

Hebrews 12.28, Weym.

Ezek. 44.3: *It is for the Prince.*

THIS came to me this morning as a word not only for the gate referred to here, but also for everything. This service, whatever it may be, this that I have to offer, all I am, and have, and want to be — *it is for the Prince.*

> "To each is given a bag of tools,
>   An hour-glass, and a book of rules;
>   And each must build ere his work be done,
>   A stumbling-block or a stepping-stone."

Our bag of tools — our body with all its various powers, the "tools" God has given us to use; the hour-glass — time; the book of rules — our Bible; the stumbling-block — that which will hinder others; the stepping-stone — that which will help them nearer Heaven — so far all is clear.

Is this clear too? We cannot build both stumbling-block and stepping-stone. We must choose which we will build. Once built it stands; we cannot pull it down and begin over again. Is not this an awful truth? Think of what it would be if, when the day is over and the work is done, we looked at it and saw a stumbling-block. God save us from that.

Every true, loving, faithful thought, word, deed, helps to build the stepping-stone. Every untrue, unloving, unfaithful thought, word, deed, helps to build the stumbling-block over which others will fall.

God help us all to build stepping-stones.

This morning, with the unexpectedness of a revelation, a question flashed through my mind: Have we any prayer like "Use me, O Lord", in the Bible? We have it in hymns; I expect we have often prayed to be used. But as I looked through my Bible for an answer to this strange question, I could not find any such prayer anywhere.

The word in 2 Timothy 2.21 simply says that if the vessel. be clean it will be ready for the Master to use; and in Isaiah 6, the "Send me" was in answer to the question, "Who will go?"

It is at least interesting and suggestive to find many other verbs occurring in prayer, Teach me, lead me, bless me, and so on, and not this verb which we would naturally expect. Is it that there is no need for it? If the vessel be clean and ready to hand, the Master will use it. It is not necessary that it should ask Him to do so. The Captain will use the soldier if he be prepared for use; words of beseeching on the soldier's part are not required. The one thing that matters is that we should be usable.

1 Kings 20.39, 40.

On March 3rd 1893 I sailed for Japan. Just before I sailed someone told me that she never knew anyone for

whom more people had prayed, and I remember feeling
startled and afraid, as well as grateful. I knew it must
mean that God knew there was very great need to pray, for
God does not waste His children's prayers; and I realized
then, more than ever before, how terrible it would be to
live an ordinary life — content with ordinariness — to be
busy here and there, and lose the thing committed to me.

Only one life, only one handful of days, and each day
counted, each hour in each day counted; what if one were
to be lost? "And as thy servant was busy here and there,
he was gone." As Thy servant, O Heavenly Master, was
busy here and there upon things that do not matter, this gift
of Thine, of time and strength to serve Thee, was gone.
Once more I say, God save us from that.

But not one of us need be discouraged. "With Thee is
forgivingness".[1] Each day brings us, like a new gift, a quite
new opportunity. Our precious handful of days may be
partly or almost wholly spent, but God does not, as earthly
masters often do, pay off a worker saying, "You are no use
to me now"; He gives us each day a new chance.

[1]Psa. 130.4, Kay.

Ruth 1.21: *The Lord hath brought me home again empty.*

Do you remember these desolate words of poor Naomi's?
Sometimes at the end of a day or a week, when we look
back, we do not see anything but a sort of emptiness. We,
too, feel like saying, "I have returned again to Thee, my
Master, but I have returned empty; I have nothing to offer
Thee." Naomi did not see how God had filled her hands,
just as the priests' hands were filled with the wave offering.[1]
She had not returned home empty; she had Ruth, the ances-

tress of our Lord Jesus. Perhaps it is sometimes so, even when we feel our days most empty. Perhaps "the God of all grace"[2] has put something into them which we do not see. They are not empty days to Him, and He in love accepts that which in love He gave.

[1]Lev. 8.26-28.   [2]1 Pet. 5.10.

If we are to recognize and obey our Lord's wishes as to every detail of service, we must often, each one of us apart, ask Him to search the ground of our heart. It is so easy to slip into wanting to serve in the way that we like best. This is service rendered, but not in God's way. Many a time I have read these words,

> "Across the will of nature
>   Leads on the path of God;
> Not where the flesh delighteth
>   The feet of Jesus trod",*

and have thought how much easier it is to write such words, or read them, or quote them, than it is to live them. But never once has our Master promised that we shall be allowed to choose our way of service, and we are trusted to trust without explanation.

1 Sam. 10.7: *Do as occasion serve thee; for God is with thee.*

It is written of a man who should have been a leader and

*Ter Steegen.

helper of others, that "he was one of those men who sweep so many small things into the field of vision that the big things are crowded out." Do not be like that. Be faithful about the small things of life, but do not let the small dominate you. If you do, you will settle down into a spiritual rut; your mind will not be open to new light; the call of a new occasion will find you unready. We are meant to be flexible in the hand of our God.

None of us have any idea of what the next step in our lives will be: Saul had not, as the story in 1 Samuel 9 and 10 shows. There may be calls upon us about which we know nothing till suddenly they come. As in Bible days, a call often comes to us to make some new decision which demands steadfast and courageous unselfishness, and the fortitude which flinches from nothing and goes on to the end. But just as food had been prepared and kept for Saul when his call came, so spiritual energy has already been prepared for us, that we may be strong to meet such a call and do whatever the occasion demands. And with us always is One who never turned back from any call.

Trustworthy

There is a terribly sad word in one of the old translations of Luke 12.46; it is *un-trustworthy*. "Place him [the unfaithful one] with those who are untrustworthy." The Lord's great desire is to say to each one of us at the end of the day, "Enter thou into the joy of thy Lord". It must be grief, beyond our imagination to conceive, when He has to say of one whom He died to redeem, "Place him with those who are untrustworthy." Am I trustworthy — one who is worthy to be trusted with any service, or with disappointment, with pain, with difficulty? Am I one who is worthy to be trusted with anything of any sort, without any preparation or any explanation? The Lord make us all His *trustworthies*.

Luke 19.17, R.V.: *And He said . . . Thou wast found faithful in a very little.*

It is possible to be badly tempted about everything in the past. But leaving the past, can we not, by His grace, be "faithful in a very little" today? We know we can, for we have such words as "My grace is sufficient for thee" to assure us that all we need for faithfulness will be given. So whatever our work is, even "a very little" thing, it is all right. Our Master does not ask for something we cannot offer, but just for faithfulness.

John 17.4, 6, Weym.: *I have glorified Thee on earth, having done perfectly the work which by Thine appointment has been Mine to do. . . . I have revealed Thy perfections to the men whom Thou gavest Me out of the world.*

These words of our Lord's and His "It is finished" seem to me to be among the most wonderful words ever spoken. As I thought of them, I thought of all who are doing what they may be tempted to feel are dull things, or difficult things, or things that call for boundless hope and love and patience. What will it be if at the end, by His grace, we can look back and thank Him that He allowed us to show in any little measure His perfections (His goodness, love,

beauty, strength) to others? Never, never shall we be able
to say as our Lord could, "I have . . . done perfectly the
work which by Thine appointment has been mine to do",
but, thank God, the Blood cleanseth; that is our one and
only confidence. Let us rejoice because we are allowed to
do anything, even the least thing, that has for its purpose
the glorifying of Him on earth.

> "My cage confines me round,
> Abroad I cannot fly."*

Have you ever felt caged? Do any of you feel caged
now? The need of the great dark sinful world calls to the
heart, and the duty of the day closes round and seems to
make it quite impossible to do anything for those perishing
millions. Or something as cage-like may hold us back,
inability of some sort or other; anyhow, we feel caged.

This morning a minute looking-glass, lying on the table,
caught and reflected the electric light, which was again
reflected in a mirror hanging on the wall. This in turn
threw a patch of brightness on the wall opposite. One can
easily imagine that reflected light falling on a reflecting
surface such as another mirror instead of on a dead wall.
If that happened there would be another reflection thrown
elsewhere, and so on indefinitely. As I looked at that little
unimportant piece of glass on the table, and thought of the
multiple reflections possible, it seemed to me that the cage-
bars disappeared. There are no cage-bars for light, any
more than for song. If only with unveiled face we receive
and reflect the glory of the Lord, He will cause that reflec-

*Madame Guyon.

tion to be again reflected, and so by His marvellous loving grace even we shall reach out to those to whom we cannot go.

The size of the reflecting glass does not matter — mine is only 3½ by 2 inches — but it does matter that there is nothing between it and the light, not even something as thin as a pocket-handkerchief.

"We all with unveiled face receiving and reflecting the glory of the Lord . . ."[1]

So let it be, Lord Jesus.

[1] 2 Cor. 3.18, Roth.

Phil. 2.14: *Without murmurings and disputings.*

This is one of the sword-words of the Bible. It does most truly pierce "even to the dividing asunder of soul and spirit, and of the joints and marrow, and is a discerner of the thoughts and intents of the heart."[1] What are the thoughts and intentions of my heart? A "discerner" here means a critic. What does this Critic say? If, when something has to be done which I do not like to do, I stop to argue about it, to wonder why I need do it, to wish I need not do it, in short, to murmur and dispute about it, then that true Critic says, "Your thoughts and your intentions are set on pleasing yourself, not your Heavenly Master", and it is a terrible thing when the Critic says that.

If any one of us has unconsciously slipped into this deadly habit, there is only one thing to be done if we are Christians at all, and that is to stop it. "Let him that stole steal no more",[2] not "let him steal a little less every day till he conquers the habit", but cut it off at once. And so it is here. Let him who argued argue no more, but obey. *Obey* is one of the sovereign words of the Bible. "Do all things without murmurings and disputings". "I cannot", does anyone say? *I can.* "I can do all things" — even this — "through Christ which strengtheneth me."[3]

Suppose we make up our mind to obey this word, and yet, suddenly, almost before we know, we find ourselves "arguing" again, what can we do? The moment we recognize what we are doing, we can refuse to continue. We have this power; God has given it to us. It is the power to will. We must instantly use that power, and as we use it, it will grow stronger. If we do not use it, it will grow weaker till we end in being more jelly-like than a jelly-fish. I am tempted every day and every night along this line, so I understand, and yet I know that we need not yield. We have a Saviour who is not only mighty to save, but able to keep; we have a God who worketh in us, strengthens, energizes, inspires, not only that we may *will,* but that we may *do* of His good pleasure.[4] And it is His good pleasure that we do all things without murmurings and disputings.

[1]Heb. 4.12.   [2]Eph. 4.28.   [3]Phil. 4.13.   [4]Phil. 2.13.

If after setting ourselves honestly to please our Lord by peaceful and glad obedience we still hear, as it were, voices within us, murmuring voices, what then? Do you remember how after Christian had passed through the Valley with its discouraging clouds of confusion, he was much worried by one of the wicked ones who got behind him, and stepping up softly to him, whispered many grievous words? "But Christian had not the discretion either to stop his ears, or to know from whence these whisperings came." And then a delightful thing happened. "He thought he heard the voice of a man as going before him, saying, 'Though I walk through the Valley of the Shadow of death I will fear none ill, for Thou art with me'. Then he was glad . . . because he gathered from thence that some who feared God were in this valley as well as himself."

I have found great comfort in this story. Often when disturbing voices come, they are from outside; they speak not our real desire, but what Satan wants to make us think we desire. If we are truly Christ's, old things are passed away; but Satan can show us, as it were in a looking-glass, those old things, our old self, and say, "That is *you*." But it is not. We are Christ's now. He has made us new. We do not want our own way, we want His way. Deep in our hearts we want it. These whisperings are from outside, not from inside. What is the best thing to do when they come? The man who was ahead of Christian answers that question. Will you do as he did? Affirm your faith. Put it into words and say it aloud as he did. (Or sing it. It is a very good plan to turn a sigh into a song.) Then you may help someone else, for certainly we are not alone in the valley of temptation. There is sure to be someone else not far off, and if only we conquer and sing — if only we live singing lives — we shall help those who are following after, and is not that worth doing?

But perhaps there are temptations that you fear very much, because they are so big and strong that they spring upon you and seem to tear you to pieces. They are not like whisperings so much as like lions.

The lion story that Bunyan puts some time before the whispering story has a splendid word for all such fears: "Is thy strength so small? Fear not the lions, for they are chained and are placed there for trial of faith where it is, and for discovering of those that have none; keep in the midst of the path, and no hurt shall come to thee." And Christian went on. He heard the lions roar, but they did no harm. Then he clapped his hands and went on.

I do like the "he clapped his hands"! Do not let us forget to clap our hands and go on.

"The lover thought to follow his Beloved, and he passed along a road where there was a fierce lion which killed all who passed by it carelessly and without devotion. Then the lover said: 'He who fears not my Beloved must fear everything, and he who fears Him may be bold and fervent in all things beside' ". Ramon Lull wrote those words in the thirteenth century, more than six hundred years ago; John Bunyan wrote his lion story in the seventeenth century, nearly three hundred years ago; and we know what one who never forgot the awful power of that fierce lion wrote about him in the first century: "Be sober, be vigilant; because your adversary the devil, as a roaring lion, walketh about, seeking whom he may devour: whom resist stedfast in the faith, knowing that the same afflictions are accomplished in your brethren that are in the world."[1] I think it is a great help to remember that there is nothing strange or new in our temptations. ("Think it not strange . . ."[2]) Temptation is common to man. Little child, boy or girl, man or woman, not one travels on the road from earth to Heaven without meeting the fierce lion, the roaring lion. *And yet he is always chained.* We need not be caught and torn by his claws. There is safety and there is victory in Christ for us. What is your temptation today? I know what mine is. I can hear that lion growl this very minute.

But I know there is nothing to fear. "There is a Greater with us than with him".[3] Only do not let us forget the words, *whom resist.*

[1]1 Pet. 5.8, 9.   [2]1 Pet. 4.12.   [3]2 Chron. 32.7, R.V.

To those who are sowing and who do not see the fruit of their sowing.

John the Baptist spent some time in Samaria just before he was imprisoned.[1] He witnessed to his Lord humbly, lovingly and very loyally. He spoke plainly about the importance of believing: "He that believeth on the Son hath everlasting life: and he that believeth not the Son shall not see life; but the wrath of God abideth on him."[2] These words seemed to do nothing at the time, but afterwards our Lord passed through Samaria, and found the place "white already to harvest."[3] He knew all about the faithful work of John, and He reminded His disciples of it: "One soweth, and another reapeth. I sent you to reap that whereon ye bestowed no labour: other men laboured, and ye are entered into their labours."[4] Perhaps from the Heavenly Country John saw this happy entering into his labour, but he never saw it on earth. So do not be discouraged if you see far less than you desire to see. Be faithful in the work appointed; if it be sowing, sow. The Lord of the field appoints sowing to one, reaping to another; but what does it matter who reaps if only there be a harvest?

Perhaps for years there may be no certain gathering of "fruit unto life eternal", but there comes a day when there is that indeed; and the sowers and reapers rejoice together. "Therefore, . . . be ye stedfast, unmoveable," not faltering or fearing or yielding to discouragement, but "always abounding in the work of the Lord, forasmuch as ye *know* that your labour is not in vain in the Lord."[5]   At any point in the long toil of sowing (or in the work of clearing the field of stones and ploughing it for sowing), if you look up you will meet the eyes that watched John sow and the love that did not forget.   Perhaps you will even hear the very words spoken to that sower, "Blessed is he, whosoever shall not be offended in Me."[6]

[1]John 3.23 ff.   [2]v. 36.   [3]Ch. 4.35.   [4]vv. 37, 38.
[5]1 Cor. 15.58.   [6]Matt. 11.6.

Neh. 4.21: *So we laboured in the work . . . from the rising of the morning till the stars appeared.*

Not "so we loitered" or "talked".   They had said, "Let us rise up and build."   If a man did not work hard, he was singled out as unusual.   In the list of honourable names in chapter 3, there is a little sentence that I am sure the men in question would like to take out of the Bible.   But they cannot.   They are for ever held up to derision and shame.   They lost their chance, the great chance of their lives; it never came again.   They "put not their necks to the work of their Lord."[1]

How glad all the other builders must have been when the wall was joined together; each set of people had done their bit faithfully, "for the people had a mind to work."[2]   And how astonished they would be to hear that their names were written in a Book that would be treasured to the end of time.

A greater than Nehemiah commissions His builders today. He notices whether we labour or loiter.   He is pleased when

we work faithfully. Let us please Him today. This day
will never come again.

Make us Thy labourers,
Let us not dream of ever looking back.
Let not our knees be feeble, hands be slack;
Oh, make us strong to labour, strong to bear,
From the rising of the morning till the stars appear.

Make us Thy warriors
On whom Thou canst depend to stand the brunt
Of any perilous charge on any front;
Give to us skill to handle sword and spear,
From the rising of the morning till the stars appear.

Not far from us those stars —
Unseen as angels and yet looking through
The quiet air, the day's transparent blue.
What shall we know, and feel, and see and hear,
When the sunset colours kindle and the stars appear?

[1]Neh. 3.5.   [2]Neh. 4.6.

Matt. 5.41: *And whosoever shall compel thee to go a mile,
go with him twain.*

I think this is the sum of our Lord's thought about willing
help to others, just as Psalm 40.8 is about joyful service:
"I delight to do Thy will, O my God: yea, Thy law is within
my heart." It is Duty that compels us to go the first mile.
How often our Lord used the word *must*. Duty may sound
a cold word to some, but that is only because it is so often

used in a cold hard way. It is really neither. The love of Christ constraineth me to run the first mile. The second mile is the overflow of love, that which need not be done, but which love loves to do.

What a very lovely thing life is when everyone runs the second mile. But do not forget the first.

There is just one power which can enable us to run the first mile — "Love is the fulfilling of the law".[1] There is just one power which can enable us to run the second mile — "I pray that your love may abound yet more and more".[2]

So let us open our hearts wide to love. Love is the mightiest thing in all the world. Love makes us to love and to do. God is Love. I can do all things through Love which strengtheneth me.

Do you remember the story of a man who desired that our Lord would come to his house for food?[3] I suppose there was plenty of food on the table, but something was forgotten. There was not enough love in that man's heart to cause him to remember the little things of love. "Thou gavest Me no water for My feet: . . . thou gavest Me no kiss." Has our Lord Jesus ever had to say words like that to us? He counts what we do or leave undone to another as something done or left undone to Him. "Inasmuch as ye have done it . . . Inasmuch as ye did it not . . ."[4] tells us that.

There is a beautiful Hebrew word translated "love" in our Authorized Version which means "to carry in the bosom". "Yea, He loved the people" (Deut. 33.3, the only time it is used). It reminds us of that dear word in Mark 9.36 about our Lord's gathering a little boy "in His arms", and not just letting him stand beside Him; he might have been shy standing there, the only child among grown-up people.

Such words tell of the Second Mile of love. "Beloved, let us love".

[1]Rom. 13.10. [2]Phil. 1.9. [3]Luke 7.36 ff. [4]Matt. 25.40-45.

1 Thess. 1.3: *Your work of faith, and labour of love, and patience of hope in our Lord Jesus Christ, in the sight of God and our Father.*

Way understands the whole to mean, "Your work inspired by faith, your toil born of love, your strong endurance which leans on the hope that waits for the Coming of our Lord, Jesus the Messiah, waits as in the very presence of God our Father."

"In Scripture every little daisy is a meadow", Luther used to say. If he had had all the helps to understanding it that scholarship gives us now, how much more he would have said it. This flower from this letter is indeed a meadow. May the Lord open its riches to us, and help us to live that life, "in the very presence of God our Father", even today. I have been specially helped by the emphasis on hope, for I have been hearing one of those things which drain human hope. But here we have words that are not mere words, but spirit and life, and as we let them bring their power to bear upon us, they create in us that which they describe.

"Your toil born of love" is beautiful, too. May these words speak with comfort, and may all we do be inspired by the faith that is fully persuaded that what He has promised, He is able also to perform.[1]

There is another comforting thought in this first letter of the first missionary. The letter is full of the lovely spirit of a love that makes these to whom he writes his own, his "ownest of owns".* Read with this in mind, the letter opens its inmost heart as a moon-flower opens its pure heart even as we watch it. And this is the comfort I see: The more this spirit of "own-ness" is given, the less those human longings pull, which for some of us can be so weakening because so painful. The old love abides, but the new dominates.

This love is of God, not of us — "Thine handmaid hath not any thing in the house".[2] It flows straight from the heart of God. It is the final confirmation of our call. To some it comes more quickly than to others, but if the heart be open to its inflow, it does come in the end. The sign of its coming is an inability to talk or write of the faults of others, except for a reason that will bear the scrutiny of our Lord Jesus. Easy talking, easy writing, is quite impossible. The wrong is seen (Divine love is never blind), but love loves the unlovable. That is the hall-mark of love, and only those to whom it has been given can take a share in any difficult work, for no others can be counted on to carry a burden without being burdened. This love makes that possible.

Is it not good to know that He who gave that love to St. Paul can give it to us? Our Forest river fills not only the beautiful Pool, but the least little crevice of the least little rock that lies in its corner. O river of the mighty love of God, pour into and fill every crevice of our being. Give it to us to love as this lover of souls loved when he wrote this great love-letter. "Being affectionately desirous of you, we were willing to have imparted unto you, not the gospel

---

*This message was written for those who had recently come out to the mission field. "Ownest of owns" is the rendering of a much-loved Tamil expression.

of God only, but also our own souls, because ye were dear
unto us."[3]

[1]Rom. 4.21.   [2]2 Kings 4.2.   [3]1 Thess. 2.8.

1 Thess. 5.14: *Admonish the unruly, comfort the timid,
sustain the weak, and be patient towards all.* Weym.

*Keep a check upon loafers, encourage the faint-hearted,
sustain weak souls, never lose your temper with anyone.*
Moff.

*Admonish those who will not conform to discipline,
encourage the sinking hearts, reach a helping hand to the
weak; be forbearing with all.* Way.

*Admonish the disorderly, soothe them of little soul,
help the weak, be longsuffering towards all.* Roth.

Each of these renderings throws a ray of light on the
Authorized Version.

It is evident that there were unruly, lazy, tiresome, weak
people then, just as there are now, and they were as trying
to faith and to good temper then as they are now. There
is nothing flabby in these directions about how to deal with
them, but I have been saved from mistake by that gentle
word, "Soothe them of little soul". Then comes something
which is far more searching than at first sight one would
suppose: *See that none render evil for evil.*[1] This has pull-
ed me up often. Unruliness, unreasonableness, unmanner-
liness, even more than some things which may be worse,
have a curious power to ruffle the spirit, unless it dwells
deep in the love of God. There is also the negative evil of a
lack of faith and hope. *To fail so, is to render evil for evil.*
Some of us may not at present be tried in this way, but

from time to time we all hear of those who are.   There is a
sympathy that weakens, and another that braces.   Which of
the two we have to offer depends on how much we know of
the spirit of our Lord.

[1]*v.* 15, A.V.

Matt. 20.27, 28:   *Whosoever will be chief among you, let
him be your servant: even as the Son of man came not
to be ministered unto, but to minister, and to give His
life a ransom for many.* (Gr. "servant" = *bondslave*.)
John 13.14, 15:   *If I then, your Lord and Master, have
washed your feet; ye also ought to wash one another's
feet.   For I have given you an example, that ye should
do as I have done to you.*

The more one reads of the history of the first century the
more amazing these words become.   We have nothing to
compare with what the word "bondslave" then connoted;
even the prodigal son, in his most abject moment, did not
use it.   But our Lord did again and again.

For He knew that just as we can never lead anyone
higher up the hill than we are willing to go ourselves, so
we can never lead them lower in humble service than we
have gone, and are willing to go again, and to continue to
go.   "He riseth from supper, and laid aside His garments;
and took a towel, and girded Himself."[1]   He had laid aside
His glory to be born in Bethlehem.   But no one in that
room had seen that; because this was seen, it helped.   That
towel — could they ever forget it?   Years afterwards one
of them remembered, saw it all again and wrote of "the
apron of humility".[2]   Surely there were tears in his heart
when he wrote.

"Now the God of patience and consolation grant you to be like-minded".[3] Let this mind be in you, which was also in Christ Jesus: Who, being in the form of God, took upon Him the form of a *bondslave*.[4]

[1]John 13.4.　[2]1 Pet. 5.5, Moff.　[3]Rom. 15.5.　[4]Phil. 2.5-7.

Luke 9.62: *No man, having put his hand to the plough, and looking back, is fit for the kingdom of God.*

This word came to me with an entirely new force a few days ago. I think I had always read it as if it referred to a turning back from the appointed path, and it is often read so. But our Lord says nothing of *turning* back. He says *looking* back. I believe there is an eternal truth contained in His choice of that verb. If the plougher, even while his feet are still following the plough, looks anywhere but straight forward, his furrow goes crooked.

The devil, as we know, has read the Psalms. We may be fairly sure he has read the Gospels. Whether he has or not, he certainly knows the peril that lies in the backward look. So he is continually trying to persuade us to look back. He delights to engage our thoughts with ourselves, our sins, our worthlessness, our failures, for when we are so engaged, we are looking back, and our furrow goes crooked at once. This is a backward pull which greatly hinders straight ploughing, and Paul was thinking of it when he wrote about "forgetting those things which are behind, and reaching forth unto those things which are before". Phil. 3.13.

Or perhaps we cannot have something we want, and do not quite understand why we cannot have it. This word meets us there. It says, Do not let your thoughts linger about the thing which you want to have. (This is a matter of the will.) Fix your desires on the track ahead. Look on. Go on.

In the context, the looking back refers to that pull of the human, which in itself is a beautiful thing, but which, *when it interferes with our vocation,* is a deadly thing. As long as there is the inward reserve, the *But* of an affection or desire which crosses the call of our Lord, we cannot possibly plough a straight furrow. "O God, my heart is fixed",[1] wrote the Psalmist. May God give us the heart that is fixed, and keep us with our eyes on the track, not looking to the right or the left or backward, but ploughing a straight furrow.

If anyone feels, as I did, smitten and penetrated by the force of those two words, *looking back,* I think you will find cheer from Psalm 25.15: "Mine eyes are ever toward the Lord: for He shall pluck my feet out of the net." How often, perhaps almost before we knew it, we have looked back; how often we have found ourselves caught in a net of longing. There is one way of deliverance: "Mine eyes are ever toward the Lord". If only that be so, then not backward longings, not discouragements because of past failure, but the loving-kindness of the Lord will be before our eyes.[2] "The Lord is my strength and my shield; my heart trusted in Him, and I am helped: therefore my heart greatly rejoiceth; and with my song will I praise Him."[3]

So, like all the words of the Lord Jesus, this word goes deeper and deeper the more one thinks of it. All know this temptation, and our Lord, who was tempted in all points like as we are, must have known it too. But He never yielded. "Therefore have I set My face like a flint".[4] And, just before He warned others against looking back, it is written of Him, "He stedfastly set His face to go to Jerusalem".[5]

[1]Psa. 108.1.   [2]Psa. 26.3.   [3]Psa. 28.7.   [4]Isa. 50.7.
[5]Luke 9.51.

*The golden dawn of a day lately brought me a new thought. It was one of those dawns that bathe the world in brightness. The air was "pure gold, as it were transparent glass";[1] the forest on the southern side was a forest of golden trees, the leaves were flakes of gold, and on one tree the little fruits that hung there were golden balls. To the east there was as yet nothing of the sun, only the loveliness of that golden dawn, but all the beauty and the gladness came from his flaming fire.

His ministers a flaming fire.[2] I had thought often of the force of that word, the burning energy, the purging purity of flaming fire, but not of this gentler ministry, this bathing in brightness all that it touches.

The first part of that verse is this: *Who maketh His angels spirits* (Hebrew, *winds*). An old Jewish legend says that His angels are as the wind going and coming and ceasing to be when their service is accomplished; selfless servants (whoever saw a wind?); obedient, whether calm or stormy, "fulfilling His word"; free (free as the wind, we say).

Is it not a perfect picture of what we want to be? selfless, obedient, free because obedient, bathing in brightness all that we touch. Only love can be that and do that. Lord, evermore give us this love.

[1]Rev. 21.21.   [2]Psa. 104.4.

*Written from the Forest.

Redeemed by His sufferings. Gal. 3.13.
Renewed by His Spirit. Titus 3.5, 6.
Rewarded by Himself. Phil. 3.7-14.

Redeemed by His sufferings. The Moravians in one of their litanies prayed to be delivered from all coldness to His death and passion. Let us pray that prayer often.

Renewed by His Spirit. Is anyone being tried by a tired dullness and heaviness? There is release in the quick look to Him, the look which does in truth believe that He will keep His word to us. Have we any cause to doubt Him? Our hearts answer, "No, not one",

> "For, loving, Thou dost love unto the end.
>   O great and dear Renewer, we have proved
>   What Love Divine can spend
>   On Its beloved."

I have learnt more of that blessed overwhelming Love lately than I can ever tell. But can we not each say the same about every month of every year since first He made us His?

And *Rewarded by Himself* — though what is there to reward? Like the priest in the old days we hold out empty hands, and ours are filled and we offer what He gives; that is all.[1] And then, the Giver rewards those to whom He gives, as though the gift were theirs. It is the last word in love, undeserved, boundless, eternal. What a life, and what a Lord!

[1]Exod. 29.24-28.

CHAPTER 10

"THAT THOU . . . MIGHTEST WAR
A GOOD WARFARE"

1 Timothy 1.18

SOMEONE has said, "It really does not matter what part of the firing line a man is in, if only he stands firm." These words have come to me today and helped me, so I pass them on to you. Such words are like a torch passed from hand to hand.

Do not let us ever forget that we are in the firing line and should not be surprised at anything that happens in the way of hindrance and trouble. The following words from M. Coillard have often come to me. He is speaking of the evangelization of the world: "It is a desperate struggle with the prince of darkness, and with everything his rage can stir up in the shape of obstacles, vexations, oppositions and hatred, whether by circumstances or by the hand of man. It is a serious task. Oh, it should mean a life of consecration and faith."

What is my part of the firing line? Each of us has a part chosen for us by the great Captain, and measured out for us too. It may be apparently out of the firing line, but it is truly in it, and each one is given just one thing to do whatever happens, and that is to stand firm.

These words (from one of Mr. Churchill's speeches in 1940), like the words of all great men, will help us who are pledged to the war that is nearest to the heart of God,

if only we ponder them and by His grace live them out:
"Bearing ourselves humbly before God, but conscious that
we serve an unfolding purpose, we are ready...." Day by
day His purpose is unfolding. "Bearing ourselves humbly
before God," let us be ready to do whatsoever our Lord
the King shall appoint.[1]

"Therefore, . . . dearly beloved and longed for, my joy
and crown, so stand fast in the Lord, my dearly beloved."[2]

[1] 2 Sam. 15.15.   [2] Phil. 4.1.

Psa. 71.3: *Be Thou my strong habitation, whereunto I may
continually resort: Thou has given commandment to save
me; for Thou art my rock and my fortress.*

That word *continually* is a great comfort. God knows
that for most of us life is no picnic, but a hard battle,
sometimes a fierce battle, and not once or twice but very
often we need a strong habitation, a rock and a fortress to
which we can fly in moments of danger; and so we have
this word which assures us of something that we desperately
need and cannot do without.

I remember once feeling too cast down and too ashamed
to "resort" to my Strong Habitation. After such a defeat as
I had just then experienced, the only possible thing seemed
to be to stay away for a while. It seemed almost wrong to
go back at once, just as if nothing had happened; and then
a child did something wrong and would not come to me
but stayed away miserably, and suddenly I understood that
the greatest wrong we can do to Love is to stay away. So
thank God for His word *continually.*

One day lately I was thinking of some who have hard
battles to fight, and the words Rotherham uses in translating

Psalm 71.4 turned into a prayer for them: "O my God, deliver me [deliver them] from the hand of the lawless one, from the clutch of the perverse and ruthless one;" and just then the bells rang out,* "God is my strong salvation," and with that came this from the previous verse, "Thou hast given commandment to save me".

Is any merry? let him sing. Is any tempted? let him affirm, *Thou hast given commandment to save me.* You are your Father's child. Look straight up to Him and say, not once or twice but many times, "Thou hast given commandment to save me".

Psa. 143.9, R.V. (mar.): *Unto Thee have I hidden.*
Psa. 83.3: *They have taken crafty counsel against Thy people, and consulted against Thy hidden ones.*

Yesterday a lovely little parable was brought to me. It did not open to me at once. At first I only saw a mango leaf. Then I saw what looked like a morsel of asparagus fern lying on either side of the midrib of the leaf. And then, at last I saw that the ferny thing was a caterpillar. Straight through its length ran a white line exactly like that white midrib; and it lay on the leaf in such a way that its white line and that of the leaf appeared to be one, and its fernyness was one in colour with the mango green. It was out in the open, and its foes, the birds (who would have enjoyed devouring it), were flying here and there, but hardly could it have been seen, it was one with its leaf, and therefore hidden by that oneness with the leaf unto which it had

*The verse of a hymn is played on the tubular bells in Dohnavur at 6 a.m., 1 p.m. and 9 p.m.

hidden. "Unto Thee have I hidden." Thou art my Leaf;
what can the powers of the air do against Thy hidden one?
These were the words that came as I looked at the living
fern on the leaf. I had thought, "Oh, to be hidden like
that, so that when the tempter comes, he would hardly see
me, but only my mighty Defender, and seeing Him, depart."
And then His own word came in answer, *Unto Thee have I
hidden* — "unto Thee", as that frail creature is "unto" its
leaf, made like unto it, colour for colour, line for line.

If one touches this caterpillar or tries to lift it up, it first
ruffles its ferny processes, and then kicks hard at both head
and tail end. As soon as ever it is left in peace it settles
down as it was before, its white line exactly on the line of
the leaf's midrib. And there it lies, fixed. It is a wonderful
thing to see, and I think the blindest could hardly fail to see
more than just a caterpillar on a mango leaf.

Has the devil got at me in spite of everything? Then
Resist[1] is the word. He prefers us to argue, to wonder why,
to discuss matters, to pity ourselves because we are being
tormented by him, to do anything but resist. And having
resisted (it is promised that he will flee if we do that) let
us follow the caterpillar's example and settle down again
in peace. There is nothing like being fixed on our Leaf,
and fixed the right way, too, no cross-purposes, but the line
of our will running on the line of our God's. That matter
of identity of line seems to be an important affair for both
caterpillars and souls. Oh, *rest in the Lord*.[2]

But we can go further than the caterpillar — as soon as
we are at rest again, we can sing. *My heart is fixed, O
God, my heart is fixed: I will sing.*[3] There is a Heavenly
power in Heavenly song.

[1]Jas. 4.7.   [2]Psa. 37.7.   [3]Psa. 57.7.

This is a Crusader story: Behind the soldiers was the sea. Before them an unknown land, where weariness, hardships and battles awaited them. Their leader knew that if things were very difficult, they would be tempted to re-embark in their boats drawn up on the shore. He did not want them to have any way of retreat, so he told them to burn their boats.

There was a day when Philip of Macedon, Alexander the Great's father, did something like that. His soldiers were storming a walled city, and lest they should give way and give up, he had the storming ladders taken away from behind them. They had to conquer or die.

Have we any boats unburnt? any ladder not flung down? In my inmost heart, do I feel, "If things get too hard, I have *that* to fall back upon; I am a soldier, yes, but I am not out for the hardest of all, the life that has no way of escape held in reserve from the most our Captain can ask from me"? If I am honest, must I say something like that? Or have I burnt my boats and flung my ladders to the ground?

Boats and ladders — what are they? *They are ways of retreat from difficult things, from fights with the great enemy of souls.* For example, if I am hardpressed and grumble, and then make excuses instead of fighting through, I am climbing down the ladder set against the city wall; I am pushing off in my boat; I am escaping from the conflict.

Sometimes a feeling, a weak, cowardly feeling, can be like retaining a boat or a ladder. If we try to evade a call to a fresh duty, or shirk an unpleasant task; or if perhaps when doing it, we hope inwardly for a way of escape, there is no victory for us till we burn that boat, fling down that ladder, and throw our whole heart into joyful obedience.

Victory on our little inner field is the best preparation for victory on the great outer field in which, in one way or another, we all hope to fight. Do we want to hasten the crowning of our Lord Jesus Christ? Then let us burn our private boats and fling down our ladders, and say, *Anything, Lord Jesus — anything.* If we do that, the day will come when we shall add another word, *Anywhere, Lord Jesus — anywhere,* and of boats and ladders there will be not one.

Eccles. 8.8: *There is no discharge in that war.*

One evening I turned to the Strong for strength and was given this with such healing power that I must pass it on. Perhaps somewhere is one for whom it is meant. First in Rotherham: "There is no furlough in war". No day, no hour, no minute when we can count on being out of reach of the fiery darts. Greek fire, as the Crusaders called it, used to terrify them because it burned on the water. There was no escape from it. There is no escape for us from the Greek fire of the enemy of souls. We have never been promised such escape. "There is no furlough in war". "If ye trust not surely ye cannot be trusted!"[1] If we let our hearts ask for what is not promised — furlough from war —; if we let ourselves wish for it; if the immost thought in us longs for respite from the conditions of war, or wonders why they are what they are, or why they are so prolonged; then we are not trusting, and we cannot be trusted with the spoils of battle — treasures for others. If this were the last word it would leave us cast down, not strong, not uplifted; but it is not the last word. "Trust ye . . . and ye shall be trusted".[2] Oh, thank God for that last word. It assures of victory over all the power of the enemy — even his Greek fire — for never does our God deceive by a mirage, and that which He commands, He enables us to do.

After the words about trusting the Lord our God, and being trusted by Him, comes this: "He appointed singers unto the Lord, and that should praise the beauty of holiness, as they went out before the army, and to say, Praise the Lord; for His mercy endureth for ever. And when they began to sing and to praise, the Lord set ambushments against [them] . . .: and they were smitten." Is it not splendid, and just like our God, to set us singing as soon as He has taught us afresh to trust? And who should sing if we cannot? Who has such a God as ours? Think of Him saying to us who are dust of the earth, Trust Me, and ye shall be trusted — trusted with the blessing of the unoffended. The fiery darts fall harmless when they strike not us but the shining shield of faith. We know these words are true, for we have proved them. Have we not proved them many a time?

So, where the inner life of the spirit is concerned, the good fight of faith is a refusal — a refusal to be drawn out from behind our shield; a refusal to allow our hearts to wonder why certain things are allowed to be; a refusal to be dissatisfied with His ways. And as in that war of olden days, when we begin to sing and to praise, the Lord sets ambushments.

These words that I have been writing are words of vital present help. We know what it is to be assaulted in a place where we were given the victory before, and we know what it is to be disappointed, and perhaps surprised, that we should be attacked *there,* in the very place where we thought we had come through. Our wonderful Bible meets this mood, as it does every other mood, with an understanding word. Jehoshaphat is speaking to his God and he tells Him the enemy has come "to cast us out of Thy possession, which Thou hast given us to inherit"[3] — "Thy possession which Thou didst cause us to possess" (Roth.).

This peace, something we could not possibly have given to ourselves, He gave it to us. It was His possession ("My peace I give unto you"). He caused us to possess it, and now the enemy has come up to cast us out of this that He has given. But shall he? Can he? If he finds us out of the place of trust and song, he can and he will. But if we are within it, if we want to be within it, then he cannot drive us out of the possession that the Lord of peace did cause us to possess. "Thanks be to God, which giveth us the victory through our Lord Jesus Christ."

[1] Isa. 7.9, Roth.   [2] 2 Chron. 20.20, Roth   [3] 2 Chron. 20.11.

Deut. 20.1-9.

These verses make it clear that there are some who are not ready for battle. They will only weaken others. The one who is thinking of something else, and wanting to do it — he cannot fight. He is not heart-whole. The man who is afraid of being asked to do hard things — "let him go and return unto his house, lest his brethren's heart faint as well as his heart." *v.* 8.

These words have power to search us all. I write that which I have proved. Are any of us today sorely tempted to wish we were doing something else? Are we afraid of something that may be asked of us? Does it seem impossible to do *that* joyfully? Do our hearts faint as we think of it? There is nothing for it but sheer honesty — the honesty of the Scriptures: "My flesh and my heart faileth".

And yet we want to fight the battles of our Lord; we want to be able to pray, vitally, effectively; we want to be so clear of self, and the desires of self, so ready for anything, that our God will not fear lest our influence weaken others; then let us finish the sentence: "My flesh and my heart faileth: *but God is the strength of my heart, and my portion for ever.*"[1] Oh, how can we ever thank Him enough for that *"but God"?* We need not go and return to our house, we will trust and not be afraid: for the Lord Jehovah is our Strength and our Song: He also is become our Salvation.[2]

[1]Psa. 73.26.   [2]Isa. 12.2.

Psalm 60.

There is often buried treasure in the headings of the Psalms. A great story is told in a few words. This is one of these stories. In the great battle of the Valley of Salt, Joab wheeled round and defeated 12,000 Edomites; and David, apparently watching that mighty charge, sang a song that was afterwards known as a "golden Ode", "a precious Psalm"[1] (like Psalms 16 and 56-59). In looking up the various translations, I found this for verse 4: "Hast Thou given Thy worshippers a flag, only that they may fly from the archers?" It is a great question. Sometimes in a very special way we are facing trial of spirit, and the tendency of the soul is to escape from that trial. But just as Joab wheeled round and faced those massed Edomites, so must we, so shall we by the grace of God, for to ask the question "Hast Thou given us a flag, only that we may fly from the archers?" is to answer it. Of course He has not given us a flag so that we might turn our backs to our enemies. Of course, then, we shall face them. Let us take victory, not defeat, for granted. This is what is meant by the words, "More than conquerors".

"Who will bring me into the strong city? . . . Wilt not Thou, O God . . .?" But sometimes the way seems long. We do not immediately find ourselves there. The way into Petra was long, over a mile long, and in parts it was almost dark because of great overhanging rocks. It was winding, too, not a straight course; and it was dangerous, for at any moment a foe might spring out from behind a shoulder of rock. There was no promise then, there is none now, of a short trial of faith and an easy winning of the fortress. But just where this cleft in the mountains opens, there were masses of deep rose-pink oleanders, and they grew about twenty feet high. So God cheers us on our way. Let us look out for the oleanders.

I shall never forget the joy with which I found, in an old book, a map of Petra and discovered, what was to me quite a new geographical fact, that there was only one way into that fortress, that strong city. Since then travellers have photographed the wonders of it, and we are familiar with every corner and every lovely colour too. But do not let us forget its amazing geography, and what it must have been to soldiers of olden time to contemplate taking it. Ever since I found that map I have thought of Petra as a synonym for the impossible — the humanly-speaking impossible.

Is there something in your life today that seems to you impossible? impossible to bear? impossible to do? Does victory there appear to be entirely impossible? Think of David's song, not when the battle was over and the victory won, but while the issue of the fight was still uncertain. That song was a song of faith, not of sight. We may have been defeated before. If so, verses 9, 10 and 12 have a word of innermost comfort. We may seem to have been "cast off" — though indeed we never were — but now the song of faith rings out triumphantly, "Who will bring me into the strong city? who will lead me into Edom? Wilt not Thou, O God . . .? Through God we shall do valiantly: for it is He that shall tread down our enemies."

[1]See A.V. mar., Young and Roth.

2 Sam. 23.9-12.

Have you ever felt, "I have had enough of fighting; I want a lull; I want peace from turmoil"? If so, read this story about Eleazar, one of David's mighty men, who, when he was left alone (for the men of Israel were gone away), arose and fought "until his hand was weary, and . . . clave unto the sword" (he was too tired to do anything but just hold on). Read also of Shammah, another warrior, who, when the Philistines were gathered together into a troop and the people fled, stood in the midst of a field of lentils and defended it, "and the Lord wrought a great victory."

It is true that there are battles of the spirit that must be fought and won alone, within. But it is also true that we have our Lord. Many of us do not have to fight alone even as to outward help; we have comrades who never desert us in a hard place: so we are far better off than either of those two men. Let it be written in the Book of the Wars of the Lord about each one of us as it was of Shammah, *But he stood.*

"But he stood" — O let the words
　Strengthen us in strong temptation.
Thou who art the God who girds
　Soldier-souls for their vocation,
　　Gird us now that we may stand,
　　Strengthened by Thy mighty hand.

2 Sam. 21.15, 16: *And David waxed faint. And Ishbi-benob, which was of the sons of the giant, . . . thought to have slain David.*

Ishbi-benob, the son of a giant and probably a giant himself, has been giving me a great deal to think about lately, for he is such a particularly disagreeable creature. He always chooses a time when people are tired, and then he attacks them furiously. So I do not like Ishbi-benob. To begin with, he is a deceiver. His name means, *The dweller in the mount.* He does *not* dwell there. His home is that deep abyss which we call Hell. But he comes as an angel of light, and he whispers texts sometimes, and suggests thoughts that sound humble. ("I am no use. I cannot do this work. I am a failure.") Very soon he has the poor soul he is attacking at his mercy. It was faint to begin with. It gives way unless, *unless,* it has an Abishai at hand. "But Abishai . . . succoured him [David], and smote the Philistine, and killed him." *v.* 17.

Perhaps none of the particular remarks mentioned as being the giant's favourite whispers have been tried on you. No matter. "He being girded with a new sword, thought to have slain David." He has plenty of new things to say, and he will say what he knows will cut deepest. His new sword is very sharp.

Moreover, the soul he is attacking is the soul of a soldier, not a slacker. "David went down . . . and fought . . . and David waxed faint." Whatever the weapon used, it is sure to be one which a soldier justly fears — not a little switch, but a new sword. It is very foolish to make little of the sword of Ishbi-benob. Paul did not. He never belittled his spiritual enemies. But he never contemplated being overcome. He had his glorious *Abishai,* and he counted upon Him. Abishai means, *Source of wealth.* What do I need — I, who am faint with long fighting — what is my need at this moment? "My God shall supply all your need according to His riches in glory by Christ Jesus."[1] Need of succour, need of protection, need of strength, need of courage, need of new hope, need of eternal joy — our Source of all wealth is close at hand. "We are more than conquerors through Him that loved us".[2]

"And David spake unto the Lord the words of this song in the day that the Lord had delivered him out of the hand of all his enemies: . . . The Lord is my rock, and my fortress, and my deliverer; the God of my rock; in Him will I trust: He is my shield, and the horn of my salvation, my high tower, and my refuge, my Saviour; Thou savest me from violence."[3] *Abishai* will not fail me. No, never. Let us speak unto the Lord the words of some song of joy and confidence. " I will call on the Lord, who is worthy to be praised: so shall I be saved from mine enemies."[4] And blessed be my *Abishai*; for He will never fail me nor forsake me.

[1]Phil. 4.19.   [2]Rom. 8.37.   [3]2 Sam. 22.1-3.   [4]*v.* 4.

Heb. 11.34: *Out of weakness were made strong.*

Here is another word of life and joy, and then immediately follows the warrior word, *waxed valiant in fight.* Moffatt has, "proved valiant", as though to suggest the thought of a test which proved the reality of the strength; and Way has it delightfully thus: *Were out of frailty made strong, became suddenly resistless in battle.*

Have we not all known that sudden clear deliverance from paralysing weakness; that sense of wings that lifts the soul out of the mud and the dust and the dullness; that which is meant by "became suddenly resistless in battle"? for the dark powers recognize the touch of the Lord of life on the soul they hoped to overwhelm, and they draw off.

"Were out of frailty made strong, became suddenly resistless in battle."

"When I called upon Thee, Thou heardest me, and enduedst my soul with much strength." Psa. 138.3, P.B.V.

2 Chron. 32.7, R.V.: *There is a greater with us than with him.*

2 Kings 6.16: *They that be with us are more than they that be with them.*

1 John 4.4: *Greater is He that is in you, than he that is in the world.*

There are some words in our Bible that seem to me like banners. They challenge the enemy, and he dare not defy them. But they challenge us, too. Do we believe them in spite of all appearances to the contrary? for each one of these words is rooted in eternity, looks through time and the things that are seen, stakes all on the Unseen, the Eternal.

These words gain tremendous force if we see them in their context — Assyria, Syria, Rome, or whatever it may be. They are some of my special banners when the call is to spiritual conflict for souls held fast by the power of the enemy.

Those who have stood in a Hindu temple at night, or in any way entered into the heart of things in a heathen land, know the simply awful feeling that can all but overwhelm the soul as it realizes the impact of great forces, alive and nearly almighty. In vital prayer for those who breathe that darkened air, the same sense of crushing might can be experienced. Here is a banner for such hours: "All the gods of the nations are idols[1] [thing of nought[2]]: *but the Lord made the heavens.*"

In the Name of our God — "even God, who quickeneth the dead, and calleth the things that are not, as though they were"[3] — in the Name of our God let us set up our banners.[4]

[1]Psa. 96.5.   [2]R.V. mar.   [3]Rom. 4.17, R.V.   [4]Psa. 20.5.

Psa. 57.1, P.B.V.: *Under the shadow of Thy wings shall be my refuge, until this tyranny be over-past.*

These words have been singing themselves over in my heart. There are times when we are very conscious of the tyranny that is still allowed to triumph ("An enemy hath done this"[1]).

People are just on the edge of open confession of Christ, and something pulls them back. Others all but turn to Him, then lose interest. Sometimes for His very own there are fierce onslaughts. "Everything seemed to conspire for the ruin of my faith and the death of my soul," wrote Coillard of the Zambesi about his first two years in Africa.

And even if it be not so tremendous a tyranny, some touch of it is known to us all. Circumstances occur that appear to be only harmful to plans that had seemed to the glory of God ("Satan hindered us",[2] wrote Paul about journeys to bring light to souls in darkness), or, inwardly we know what it is to have our wheels drag heavily like those of Pharaoh's chariot in the sand.

But it is all only for a moment, "Though now for a season, if need be,"[3] is Peter's heartening word. How often I have leaned my heart on that *for a season* — it is not for always. "And under the shadow of Thy wings shall be my refuge, until this tyranny be over-past."

So we shall not be shaken by any tyranny. "My heart is fixed, O God, my heart is fixed: I will sing, and give praise."[4]

What a singing life is theirs on the other side of the tyranny. Let ours be more and more like theirs. So shall that tyranny utterly fail to dominate our spirit whatever it may do to our flesh. "I will give thanks unto Thee, O Lord, . . . I will sing".[5]

[1]Matt. 13.28.   [2]1 Thess. 2.18.   [3]1 Pet. 1.6.
[4]Psa. 57.8, P.B.V.   [5]v. 10, P.B.V.

CHAPTER 11

"UNTO ALL ENDURANCE"

Colossians 1.11, Roth.

I READ this yesterday and want to pass it on. It is from one of Bishop Paget's letters to a son who was with his regiment in India and Burma. For all who are facing any sort of difficulty (and who is not?) it is a fine word:

"Life's not a level or a smooth road; but it's a blessing to breast the hills and trudge over the stones with a good heart, and I think one sometimes does one's best work on the uphill bits, though one may not know it."

Put that with these words from one of John Buchan's books which have strengthened me hundreds of times: "Have no fear. . . . You have chosen the roughest road, but it goes straight to the hill-tops." May they help us to choose the road that goes straight to the hilltops. And I would add this: "Therefore . . . with strong endurance let us race along the course that stretches before us, turning our eyes away from all else toward Jesus, to Him who gives the first impulse to our faith, to Him who brings it to final maturity." Heb. 12.1, Way.

The unusualness, the unexpectedness, of the way thoughts (and so, words) are sometimes put together in the Bible set it apart from all other books. It is to me one of the innumerable touches that tell of the Divine. No human writer would have written thus. There is an example of this in Hebrews 12.1, *"Run* with *patience"*, which is like the word in Colossians 1.11, "Strengthened with all might, according to *His glorious power,* unto [not some flashing magnificence but just] *all patience"* — and the same verse holds another of these marks of the Divine — *"longsuffering* with *joyfulness".* Which of us would have put these words together? But the Holy Spirit does.

Patience, Young says, means "endurance". Rotherham translates Hebrews 12.1, "With endurance let us be running", and so in Colossians 1.11, "With all power being empowered according to the grasp of His glory unto all endurance and longsuffering with joy".

I have been looking up the word in Young and find it comes much more frequently than the word which means only longsuffering. It is one of those trumpet-call words which sound forth a challenge and stir the heart and kindle it to rise and do. As I thought of it this morning, I knew that life can offer us no greater gift than the opportunity to learn to endure. Should we wonder then that we have this gift sometimes? Should we wonder that the soul that follows hard after our Lord does invariably find itself in need of this special virtue? Should we wonder as though some strange thing happened unto us?

And as I thought of this I found something equally joyful and inspiring: Our God has chosen this very word to describe Himself, and with that word He links another, that dear word *consolation,* which means *encouragement,* the comfort that braces the soul; He is *the God of patience and consolation* — "the God of the endurance and of the encouragement".[1] And this God is our God forever and ever.

[1]Rom. 15.5, A.V., Roth.

"Many seem patient when they are not pricked." Richard Rolle said these words about 600 years ago, and he quoted the old version of Proverbs 12.21: "Whatever happens to the righteous man *it shall not heavy him*."

I have been thinking of four of the meanings of the word translated "endure" in our Authorized Version:

To remain under, as in Matt. 10.22; Heb. 10.32; 12.2, 3; and others.

To bear up under, 2 Tim. 3.11; 1 Pet. 2.19.

To be long- or patient-minded, Heb. 6.15.

To be strong, firm, Heb. 11.27.

I wonder if these words can take to you what they brought to me, but then I remember whose they are, and know that they will find the one for whom they are sent.

Are we finding it difficult to *remain under, bear up under,* something? Does it sometimes seem impossible to be truly, and for long, *patient-minded?* Do we feel far from being *strong, firm,* as our dear Lord was all through His holy life? There is only one way of peace when we feel like that; it is to lay hold afresh on some sure word of promise or assurance. "My grace is sufficient for thee: for My strength is made perfect in weakness."[1] It is the word of Him who endured, to you and to me. It cannot fail. Our Lord said, "What things soever ye desire, when ye pray, believe that ye receive them, and ye shall have them."[2]

[1] 2 Cor. 12.9.   [2] Mark 11.24.

John 6.18, 19: *And the sea arose by reason of a great wind that blew. So when they had rowed about five and twenty or thirty furlongs, they see Jesus walking on the sea, and drawing nigh unto the ship: and they were afraid.*

The beginning of life is helped by our natural vigour and all manner of bright hopes and expectations. The end of life is lightened by the thought that it is the end. But the middle can be a difficult time. If there was glamour in our beginning, it has vanished now like the dew that has seen the sun, and sometimes a dullness creeps over the spirit there, and often the boat is distressed by the waves, for the wind is contrary.

Is it not beautiful that our Lord Jesus drew nigh unto the ship just when it had reached the middle of the Lake? (The sea of Galilee is about six miles broad at the broadest part.) Where we most need Him, there He is — there He always is — our very present Help.

"Come out of the bustlings, you who are bustled" — I came upon this in a book about the early Quakers. It is a good word for times when we are tempted to be worried about trifles; the devil delights to make us "bustled". Fuss and peace never live together.

"She endured with much patience, neither fainted nor murmured at it, for *the Lord kept her easie*" — this was written by her children of Margaret Fox, who had been imprisoned and in many ways treated unjustly and cruelly. She went through everything with amazing courage, never yielding one inch, and never flinching. This lovely little sentence explains it, "The Lord kept her easie."

Often we feel ashamed when we think of what others have suffered. Our tiny troubles seem so small, and *are* so small in comparison with theirs, that we almost hesitate to mention them to our Lord at all. And yet He knows that we need His grace for them, little though they be; and He can do for us what He did for Margaret Fox. He can "keep us easie."

2 Thess. 3.5, R.V.: *The Lord direct your hearts into the love of God, and into the patience of Christ.*

The other translations agree in this, and Way's, which is a free rendering, is: "May our Lord pilot your hearts into the haven of the love of God, into such calm patience as was Messiah's". Are they not lovely words of peace?

Is there ever a time in any life, that is wholly laid on the altar, when these words are not spirit and life? Take the picture Way suggests — the contrary winds stirred by the adversary, continually seeking to drive the ship out into disquiet; the Lord Himself as pilot, guiding it into the haven that is His own great love, into the calm patience, the endurance, of our Lord Jesus.

Then, verse 16 of this same chapter: "Now the Lord of peace Himself give you peace always by all means";[1] "in all ways and at all seasons";[2] "always, under all conditions";[3] "continually, whatever comes."[4] Each rendering adds to the force of this prayer, which is charged with effective power. *Peace* — how the word finds us where we are — peace under all conditions. May that blessed word be fulfilled in us all this day, and every day.

[1]A.V.   [2]Con.   [3]Way.   [4]Moff.

After the wicked King Louis XIV of France revoked the Edict of Nantes and condemned tens of thousands of the noblest men and women of France to torture and to death, many brave women were imprisoned in a huge tower called the Tour de Constance. The dungeon was a terrible place; its walls were 15 feet thick, and it was lighted only by narrow embrasures. The sister of a martyred minister lived for thirty-six years in that prison, and never gave way.

When at last the Huguenot women were released in 1768, someone found a word scored in the middle of the hard stone floor. The inscription is hardly readable, and to see it even on a fine summer day, one has to kneel down and have a candle lighted; otherwise it is too dark. That one word is *Resist*. It is thought that some woman carved it, perhaps with a needle (the tracing is so faint), toiling at that word to help and strengthen herself and others, so that after she was gone they might be encouraged in their resolve to endure till the end. Surely the powers of endurance that God can give to the human soul are beyond our understanding. These women had not even the comfort of their Bibles in prison. They had nothing, *nothing* — but God. Can the God who so gloriously nourished them with Heavenly strength not feed us also, in our lesser needs, as we wait day by day upon Him?

In a book translated from the Russian, the writer, a prisoner for Christ's sake, tells what a terrible place the prison was. It was called The Ship, and he says it was indeed like a ship bearing men out and away into the fearful realm of the unknown. Deep in its depths was a cellar — the place of execution. Two doors led to it. Beside those doors someone wrote in charcoal these words, "And even this shall pass."

As I have said before, when we think of suffering, such as myriads have endured in all ages, in all lands, and of the suffering, too, that many are enduring today, our own little troubles and difficulties seem too small to think about at all, and we can only find relief in praying for those who suffer. And yet, though this is so, sometimes our trifles can try us a good deal, and those words, "And even this shall pass", may perhaps bring comfort to some among us. At longest it is "but for a moment",[1] and then——?

[1] 2 Cor. 4.17.

2 Cor. 4.18:   *Not at...but at....*

I have been finding help in laying the great story of 2 Kings 6.13-17 alongside the great words of 2 Corinthians 4.8-18. An host with horses and chariots was round about the city. . . . We are pressed on every side, perplexed, pursued, smitten down at times, always delivered unto death (see R.V.). "Alas, my master! how shall we do? And he answered, Fear not: for they that be with us are more than they that be with them. And Elisha prayed, and said, Lord, I pray Thee, open his eyes, that he may see. And the Lord opened the eyes of the young man; and he saw . . . [what had been there all the time] the mountain full of horses and chariots of fire round about Elisha."

The secret of peace and courage is shown to us in this story, taken with the words that lead up to and follow after "While we look not at the things which are seen, but at the things which are not seen". So let us live, not in the visible but in the Invisible, not in the temporal but in the Eternal.

While our eyes are fixed on our troubles — "The things which are seen" — those troubles are doing nothing for us;

they are useless. But while our eyes are fixed, not on our troubles but on something beyond — "the things which are not seen" — those troubles have a wonderful power to work for us. We are not told how it is they have this power, or how they use their power, only that they have it: "For our light affliction, which is but for a moment, worketh for us a far more exceeding and eternal weight of glory; while we look not at the things which are seen, but at the things which are not seen: for the things which are seen are temporal; but the things which are not seen are eternal."

This is something we should never have discovered for ourselves, and I have often thanked God for telling us this Heavenly secret. It helps so very much in hard times. Job, and Joseph, and Moses, and Paul, and many another in Bible times, and countless numbers since then, came through hard days when crushing blows fell upon them, like wave upon wave beating on their souls. But they know now (we do not know this yet) what the exceeding and eternal weight of glory is. Are they sorry now, as they look back, that they endured? I think not.

We can only go on in peace as we see "Him who is invisible",[1] that is, as we look away from the trial to the Lord. This is what Moses did, and so he was able to endure. "Where there is no vision, the people perish".[2] If we see only the things of time, and forget the things of Eternity, we perish, our faith withers and we become weak and hopeless. We need vision for life, vision for prayer, continual undimmed vision, if we are to be those on whom our God can count for anything, any time, anywhere.

[1]Heb. 11.27.   [2]Prov. 29.18.

Heb. 12.3: *Consider Him that endured . . . lest ye be wearied and faint in your minds.*

What a word of power this is — there is uplifting in it. We look at ourselves and we go down to the lowest depths. We look at others, and — though a shining example can help — we may be cast down by the very contrast between ourselves and that which we see in them. We look at our Lord (there is no question of contrast there, for it is immeasurable); but as we look we are not cast down but marvellously lifted up. "Consider Him . . . lest ye be wearied and faint in your minds" — there is strength in that look.

Therefore it is written, "In the day when I cried Thou answeredst me, and strengthenedst me with strength in my soul."[1] There are some who are going through trial of spirit — perhaps many know of it and are helping; perhaps only the Lord Jesus knows. Either way the good word holds, *Consider Him.*

[1]Psa. 138.3.

I have been reading an Anglo-Russian woman's story. Her husband, a brave and good doctor, was shot by the Reds. She had to work hard to educate her two children. She suffered much, but she never makes much of that; she tells of the suffering of others. This is one of her stories: On the night of Easter Eve, two Christian women were to be examined by the Reds in the prison. The wardens fetched them, and as they walked along the damp, dimly-lighted, endless passages, the younger of the two — quite a young girl — remembered what night it was, and before she could be stopped, she suddenly called out in a glad, fearless voice,

"Christ is risen!", and from behind the locked doors of the cells on either side of the dark passage came the muffled answers of the prisoners, "He is risen indeed!" That young girl was locked up in a cell alone after that; later, she may have been shot, nobody knows; but surely her courage brought encouragement to others; for, "Who shall separate us from the love of Christ", the "Christ that died, yea rather, that is risen again, who is even at the right hand of God, who also maketh intercession for us"? Rom. 8.35, 34.

One of the first gold coins ever minted in England had engraved on it the cross of Christ and the motto, "It shall be lifted up in glory." It was a quarter-florin of the time of Edward III, and there was later an English gold coin called an angel, with the device of Michael the archangel trampling upon the dragon, and the words "By Thy Cross save us, O Christ, our Redeemer." Sometimes it seems long to wait till the Cross is lifted up in glory. But it will not seem long when we look back. 1 Peter 1.6 has a word of peace, "Now for *a little while,* if need be . . ."[1] I have been enjoying those words; at the most it is only "for a little while".

When Mr. Churchill was a prisoner of war he wrote of the hours crawling like a "paralytic centipede". It is generally truer to say, Time flies. Even so, I understand the "paralytic centipede" feeling, and so I expect do some of you. Lay hold then on this blessed other word, "a little while". Look beyond the feeling of the minute and rejoice because that word is true. There is something delightful, I think, in St. Paul's "Now is our salvation nearer than when we first believed."[2] Nobody can possibly upset that fact. It is as sure as that two and two make four.

[1]R.V.   [2]Rom. 13.11, R.V. mar.

CHAPTER 12

"BUT IF IT DIE"

John 12.24

1 Pet. 2.4, 5: *Chosen of God . . . to offer up spiritual sacrifices, acceptable to God by Jesus Christ.*

A "spiritual sacrifice" is something only the Lord sees. It is a kind of secret between the soul and Him. Let us offer such as we go through today, going unto the altar of God, unto God, our exceeding joy.[1]

> "O Lord, that I could waste my life for others,
>   With no ends of my own,
> That I could pour myself into my brothers,
>   And live for them alone.
>
> Such was the life Thou livedst; self-abjuring,
>   Thine own pains never easing,
> Our burdens bearing, our just doom enduring,
>   A life without self-pleasing."

I must have been about seventeen when I came upon this of Faber's, and turned it into a prayer; for it is not enough to long to live that life, it must be the very prayer of our hearts. Shall we make it our prayer today, meaning it with all that is in us? "A life without self-pleasing", Lord, this I ask of Thee, this I desire; and that which Thou findest lacking in me do Thou of Thy goodness vouchsafe to supply.

There is nothing worth doing which has not sacrifice set in its heart. We know that that word is true. But do any of you feel that "sacrifice" is too great a word for that which you can bring? But it is used not only about the offering of great bullocks, but about two little birds: "To offer a sacrifice according to that which is said in the law of the Lord, A pair of turtledoves, or two young pigeons."[2] Is not this a comforting thought? I found it so. With it came the verse from the old hymn:

> "If on our daily course our mind
> Be set to hallow all we find,
> New treasures still of countless price
> God will provide for sacrifice."*

[1]Psa. 43.4. [2]Luke 2.24.

Phil. 2.5-7: *Let this mind be in you, which was also in Christ Jesus: Who . . . made Himself of no reputation.*

Years ago I was staying with friends in Scotland. A convention was being held in the big barn (it was there Bishop Moule found fulness of life), and there were many of the Keswick speakers staying in the house. We had meals in a large dining-room, round a long table. I was one of the youngest there.

Suddenly one morning at breakfast, one of the speakers looked straight across at me, and slipping my name into the song, began to sing very loudly to the tune, "What a Friend we have in Jesus",

*J. Keble.

"Have you lost your reputation?
Are you trusting in the Lord?"

The tableful of speakers and people stopped talking to listen, and in the horror of that moment, devoutly longing to disappear under the table, I lost the next two lines. The singer went on ruthlessly, still fixing me with his great blue eyes,

"Have you found a full salvation
From what people think or say?
Do you mean to live for Jesus,
Let the world say what it may?"

By this time the others at the table, in pity, broke in upon the song, and left me to recover in peace.

But those words were unforgettable. I have lived to thank God for them, though I cannot imagine a more appalling way of conveying a spiritual truth.

Have you lost your reputation? To lose it, and to keep on being willing to lose it, for His sake and for the sake of the souls for whom He died, is to take up His cross daily. There is one way of losing our reputation which is likely to come to all who love their Lord enough, and souls enough, and that is to refuse to give weakening sympathy when it is asked for (knowing well that smooth sayings never helped a soul), and to offer instead the sympathy which braces, which says, "Think it not strange" — "Count it all joy".[1] Someone comes to us full of complainings about the hardness of things, wanting pity, wanting us, indeed, to say what Peter (Satan through Peter) said to our Lord Jesus, "Pity Thyself."[2] We may meet this poor wish in a way that sends that soul away happy (in a kind of sloppy happiness) saying, "How well she understands", "I knew he would understand". Or, if we take the other line, the *Think it not strange* — *Count it all joy* line, then (unless there is a response to the joyful call of the highest, the hardest) some-thing very different may be said; there will be talk with more "sympathetic" friends — a weak soul knows where to find weakness — and we shall lose every shred of our reputation for love and understanding.

It may take a long time to lead that soul to victory. That is where "daily" comes in. We may daily accept this for His sake.

And who would hesitate? Which is dearer to us, our reputation, or the soul for whom He died?

¹ Pet. 4.12; Jas. 1.2. ²Matt. 16.22, mar.

2 Kings 2.19-22: *Salt in the spring of the waters.*

I have noticed that when there is a word about the won-derful love of God, someone is sure to write and say how much that word helped; and this is joy to me. But I have also noticed that often that same one is cast down about the merest trifle, overwhelmed by difficulty, overcome by temptation. This should not be. The love of God is meant to make us valiant. A soldier who is constantly bemoaning difficulties has missed something.

This morning as I read 2 Kings 2, it seemed to me that verse 21 was for such: "And he went forth unto the spring of the waters, and cast the salt in there, and said, Thus saith the Lord, I have healed these waters; there shall not be from thence any more death or barren land." The salt was cast into the spring of the waters, and then the Lord said, "I have healed these waters." We must let God deal with the spring of action, the very inmost in us, if we are to be thoroughly right. What is it that makes things go wrong? It is often some inward pride. What is the cause of discontent? It is that love of myself that makes me magnify my own troubles and forget those of others. Self, self, self at the spring of the waters makes those water utterly useless for the help of others.

Salt smarts when it touches raw flesh. Do not be surprised if the first effect of some sharp word of God applied to your soul is painful. Suddenly to realize that quarrelsomeness has its root in pride; that to take offence simply means that I love myself; that laziness is another kind of self-love — is to be stung, as the raw flesh is stung if salt or anything with cleansing power be applied to it. If we ask our God to cast salt into the spring of our being, we are asking Him to deal with us thoroughly, to cleanse us thoroughly.

That means that next time the temptation comes to pride, selfishness, sloth, we claim the power of the Cleansing, and in the strength of our God refuse to yield to the *I*.

Long ago I read these words of George Herbert:

"Who goeth in the way which Christ hath gone,
Is much more sure to meet with Him, than one
That travelleth by-ways."

Are we going in the way which Christ hath gone, or are we only talking and praying and singing about it? What about likes and dislikes? what about choices? what about Self? Christ's way is the way that says "No" to the "I" that rises up so often and in many different disguises. "If any man will come after Me, let him deny himself [say "No" to himself], and take up his cross daily, and follow

Me."[1] A "by-way" is any other way, any easier way, any self-pleasing way. We shall not meet Christ if we travel in a by-way.

[1]Luke 9.23.

Many years ago a woman was sent to me to train for evangelistic work. After a few days with our Preaching Band she said with great disgust, "Always this going on! What we have done is enough."

An old book that has come down to us from the fourteenth century says, "Verily it is perilous for a soul not to seek to make any further progress." And it speaks of being in dead earnest to go on, and uses a word which sticks in the mind like a burr: "Get to thee meekness and charity, and if thou wilt, then travail and *swink* busily to have them. You shall have enough to do in getting of them."

Swink means "toil". In one sense we do not have to toil any more than the flowers of the field must toil. But in another sense, as that poor disgruntled woman said, there is always a going on, with what that implies of toil. "I press toward the mark".[1] The mark is always on before, and to press on means to *swink*.

The *I* rises up. *I* want this, *I* want that. *I* want to do this, *I* don't want to do that. *I* like this, *I* don't like that. Well, we may let that "I" rule. If so, we shall not go on, and presently we shall begin to slide back. Or, we may look to the Lord who is continually going before us (even when it is night in our soul, He shows us a light like fire) and ask Him to crucify that "I". To co-operate with Him when He does this is not always easy; the "I" is so terribly dominant. It is bound to mean *swink*.

[1]Phil. 3.14.

Matt. 16.24, 25.

In *The Pilgrim's Progress* when Christian saw the Cross, his burden loosed from off his shoulders, and three Shining Ones blessed him, and he sang a song. What did he do next? He tried to help others. Presently he came to the foot of a hill steep and high, and he set his face like a flint and began to climb that hill. Now suppose the Dream had shown him helping another up that hill, would it show him able to help that other higher than he had gone himself?

Our life, from the day when we find our burden loosed from our shoulders, to the day we hear the bells of the City ring again for joy, might be shown in a single picture, that of a climber climbing uphill and helping others to climb. And the climber would always be just a step ahead, for we cannot push people up the Heavenly hill, we can only help them if we hold out our hand and say, "Come."

Walker of Tinnevelly was seventeen when he began to climb; and for him, as for us, the hill was called Difficulty. But he pressed on. He loved the story of the Swiss guide who "died climbing". Walker died climbing.

But, put in common words, climbing means what? Sometimes it helps to say what a thing does not mean: it does not mean selfishness (a selfish Christian is an anomaly, one might as well talk of sour sugar). It means giving all, spirit and soul and body, to the obedience of Christ. For Mr. Walker it meant the yielding up of all self-choices, and every kind of softness, and of course, all sloth. It will not mean less for us. The Lord Jesus explained once for all what it meant when He said, "If any man will come after Me, let him deny himself."

Do not think Mr. Walker was always teaching and preaching. He helped in all the everyday jobs, too. Helping others to climb means doing whatever helps them most, and doing it joyfully. This is the life most worth living. This is our glorious calling. Come, then, let us climb.

Phil. 2.4, 5: *Look not every man on his own things, but every man also on the things of others. Let this mind be in you, which was also in Christ Jesus.*

"He that loveth much doeth much, and he doeth much that doeth a thing well. He doeth well that serveth more the common weal than his own weal."*

"The common weal" — God help us to serve it "with no ends of our own". This is the happy life. Nothing wrong can come to us if we have no ends of our own to serve. Nothing can really touch our happiness if we are trusting our Lord to lead us so that we shall serve the common weal. "When He giveth quietness, who then can make trouble?"[1] When He giveth happiness, who then can disturb us?

[1]Job 34.29.

"Many privily seek themselves in the things that they do, and wot not thereof. It seemeth them also that they stand in their good peace when all things fall after their will and feeling. And if it fall otherwise than they desire, they are soon moved and sorry."†

"For one look at self take ten looks at Christ." The ten are ten times as important as the one, but it is sometimes

*Thomas a Kempis.

†Thomas a Kempis.

well to take that one look, honestly, and make sure we are not doing what Thomas à Kempis's words describe. If we find we are, then there is only one thing to do — confess and turn from that hateful self-love which does so easily ensnare us; and as we look to our Saviour, whose blood cleanses from all sin, and trust Him to cleanse and keep us, we find that He who is mighty to save is also able to keep. We do not find any provision made in our Bible for a life of defeat, but there is full provision made for a life of victory over all the power of the enemy.

"Now unto Him that is able to keep you from falling, and to present you faultless before the presence of His glory with exceeding joy, to the only wise God our Saviour, be glory and majesty, dominion and power, both now and ever. Amen." Jude 24, 25.

Sometimes we suddenly recognize something in ourselves as self, self-love, self-choice, self-pity, which a year ago we should not have recognized at all. This shows that indeed our patient Lord is going on to perfect us. More light is flowing into our room and so we see the dust more clearly. Even though a pang strikes us when we see the dust, let us thank God we do see it. We should not, if it were not for His light.

In other words, *There is always something more in your nature which He wills to mark with the Cross.** If we are following hard after Him we shall be aware of this. Never a day will go by without some secret marking of the Cross deep, deep within us. And to what end? "This spake He, signifying by what death he should glorify God."[1] When thou wast young (spiritually immature) thou wouldest bitterly have resented any interference with thy liberty, thou girdedst thyself, and walkedst whither thou wouldest, there

*H. Maynard Smith, *Frank, Bishop of Zanzibar.*

was nothing trying to thee in that delightful freedom. But now, how different! Thou canst be trusted with what seems hardest to the natural bent of thy mind. Thou canst be trusted not to fail. It is those who are crucified who most clearly glorify their crucified Redeemer.

All the time I have been thinking of our Lord's far-reaching words to Peter, the thought of Philippians 3.10 has been with me. Weymouth translates it, "I long to know Christ and the power which is in His resurrection, and to share in His sufferings and die even as He died"; and Way has "the power outflowing from His resurrection".

The power makes the experience possible; the power perfects that which concerneth us. It is always first the power, then the crucified life. The God with whom we have to do is the God of limitless power. He is not going to be baffled by anything in us. It is "the power of His resurrection" that assures us that even we shall be "made conformable unto His death".

¹John 21.19.

Psa. 20.1, 3 (mar.): *The Lord . . . turn to ashes thy burnt sacrifice.*

A thing turned to ashes is utterly gone, we cannot recover it. I see in this a very deep thought of God. It is perhaps the deepest of all His thoughts for us while we are here in the flesh. It leads to the great "not My will, but Thine be done" of Gethsemane and Calvary.

Some of us are a long way from even beginning to understand this. None of us are anywhere near a full understanding, but I do want to lay these words on your hearts, even on the hearts of you who are still young. If you want to be one of those of whom the Lord can ask anything in the days to come, begin now by laying your little offerings upon His altar. Lay down your little choices, your will about very little things. He will not call these love-offerings little. He will accept them, and cause His face to shine upon you, and give you peace.

Something of this is in that wonderful word in Psalm 43.4: *the altar of God, . . . God my exceeding joy.* It is not a sad thing to be allowed to lay a sacrifice on the altar, and see it accepted and turned to ashes. It is a joyful thing; it is the most joyful thing in all the world.

The word I have for you today came to me first, to my own heart, in the early morning of Christmas Eve. It is the word *crucified.* I found it in *Daily Light*: "They that are Christ's have crucified the flesh with the affections and lusts."[1] *Crucified affections* — that pierced me.

Our days may be joyful, but even so, we shall always find something that we are meant to crucify. Does Self never rise up at such times? Self and the desires of Self? It is not easy truly to crucify the "I". As one thing after another arises, perhaps something no one else knows about, let us take it as something more to be nailed to His cross, for love of Him who loved us and gave Himself for us.

Many years ago, in my first year in India, the words, "See in it a chance to die", were spoken deep in my heart by a Heavenly Voice. They have never ceased to help me. May the Lord help us to see, in whatever makes us want to assert our "I" and its desires, a chance to crucify that rebel, in order that Christ may live in us and triumph.

[1]Gal. 5.24.

Unexpected Fellowship

"Then I was by Him, as one brought up with Him: and I was daily His delight, rejoicing always before Him".[1] Did not our Lord, the daily Delight of His Father, He who was always by Him, "leave a blank" when He came to earth? for God so loved that He gave, and to give implies a "doing without". At any rate that was how it came to me.

Think of it. It is a radiant thought. In every giving up, whether it be of those who are daily our delight, or of our own desires, for love of Him who died for us; in every little private resolve of the heart to do the thing that pleaseth Him, whatever be the cost, and to do it not with a grudging spirit but with glad abandon; in every such experience, however small, we may have fellowship with the Father and with His Son, Jesus Christ.

[1]Prov. 8.30.

Rev. 1.18: *I am He that liveth, and was dead; and, behold, I am alive for evermore, Amen.*
Heb. 7.25: *He ever liveth to make intercession for them.*

What should we do if we had not that assurance? But I do not think that I ever paused long over the three words, "and was dead", till last night. They take us straight to Calvary. I know that we may look at what those words mean in many ways, but last night it was the suffering which nothing alleviated that held my thoughts. And the cause: "That parched dry lip, that fading face, that thirst, were all for me."

From that I went on to what St. Paul calls "the fellowship of His sufferings,"[1] not avoided, but ardently desired; and that includes spiritual pain over souls — not in [illegible] so much, perhaps, as seen one by one, this one, that one, who is crucifying afresh the Son of God.

And was dead. It is the Saviour who suffered in the flesh and in the spirit, past the power of imagination to conceive, who ever liveth to make intercession for us as we share in "the fellowship of His sufferings". But let us not forget that the words "and was dead" are followed by "Behold, I am alive for evermore"; and because "He ever liveth to make intercession" for us, we may hear Him say, "I have prayed for thee".[2]

[1]Phil. 3.10. [2]Luke 22.32.

An illustration used by Captain Wallis at Keswick one year was about an apple tree. A child, in turning over the leaves of an old gardening book, read that if an apple tree did not bear fruit, a good plan was to drive a few iron nails into it. She told her father of this, and he tried it with a useless tree in his garden. Next year that tree bore prolific fruit.

Captain Wallis saw this tree, and he turned to his Lord and said, "Lord, is that the secret of my barrenness? Is that why I so often have failed in the day of testing? Is that why temptation has so easily conquered me? Is that why I have become the victim of those things which I know do not belong to the new life in Christ? Is that why so often I have failed in bearing fruit unto Thy glory? Is it because I have raised a protest against the nails being driven into this flesh-life, this wretched *ego,* this cursed self? Have I said, 'No, Lord, I do not give consent to that crucifixion'? And is this the result of all this — just barrenness?" The Lord make us willing for the nails to be driven in, "for only as we are willing to die, can we bear fruit, and live the resurrection life of the Lord Jesus Christ."

The same speaker went on to tell of a minister who was attending the Keswick Convention in the early days. At the close of one of the meetings he jumped to his feet and said, "Mr. Chairman, I long to be conformed to the will of God, and to live a life well-pleasing unto Him. But I am the victim of an enslaving habit, and I cannot give it up. If I tried to do so, I should die. What shall I do?" And the Chairman looked at him and said a word that was surely God-directed, "Then die!" It does not matter that any of us should live, but it does matter that not one of us should allow anything to interfere with our fellowship with God.

And Captain Wallis added this: "A Christian means 'Christ —' and the remaining letters 'i-a-n' simply mean '*I Am Nothing.*' Only as this is really true do we discover what Paul calls the glory of the cross."

But do not let that mean to anyone, "*I* am nothing, so it is no use expecting *me* to conquer in the fight." That is Self making weak excuses for Self. Take the words you know so well and count on their truth — I am nothing, but I am Christ's; therefore, "I can do all things [this thing that I feel impossible] through Christ which strengtheneth me." Phil. 4.13.

Last night I went to sleep resting upon two words from Psalm 73: "I am continually with Thee" and "It is good for me to draw near to God" — continually with Him, and yet needing to draw near, and still nearer. "As for me, nearness to God is my good", is Kay's version, and he quotes in a footnote, "Nearest to Thee, my God, is best."

We all know it, feel it, want it, but this morning as I read again in Revelation 1.17, "And when I saw Him, I fell at His feet as dead", the words spoke to me as though newly-written and read for the first time. May the Lord draw us into such a nearness that we shall see Him, in so far as mortals may, till all that belongs to the "I" in us falls at His feet as dead.

When General Gordon felt the uprising of that "I" in him, he used to go to his tent and shut himself in with his God. If any asked him what he had been doing, he would say, "I have been hewing Agag in pieces."

In my first year in Japan, Mr. Buxton and I were singing choruses rather joyfully as with some others we walked down the road. "I do wish you would not sing like that", said a voice behind us. Mr. Buxton looked down at me and smiled, "Good for the flesh", he said. And I have told how, many years ago, when something chilling happened, another word came — inwardly this time — "See in it a chance to die." So this verse in Revelation 1.17 was not new. What a patient God is ours. For the pieces of Agag seem to have a rather dreadful way of reviving, and there is no place where we can be sure that he will be really done to death but in the dust at the feet of our Lord Jesus. "When I saw Him, I fell at His feet as dead."

Lord Jesus, our Beloved, let us see Thee. Let all within us that would hinder, die; let it die utterly and swiftly, till there is nothing left of us but the reflection of Thy face.

Psa. 43.4: *Then will I go unto the altar of God.*

Abram's two altars. He had been defeated; there must have been a sense of loss, discouragement, deep sadness.

To one who had listened to the voice of his God it must have been a very scourge to hear the voice of a Pharaoh speaking in just rebuke. But there is no sitting down in deadly depression, no self-pity. "He went on his journeys from the south even to Beth-el, unto the place where his tent had been at the beginning, between Beth-el and Hai; unto the place of the altar, which he had made there at the first: and there Abram called on the name of the Lord."[1]

Beth-el, the House of God; Hai (Ai), a heap, a place connected later with heaped-up sin; between the two places, an altar. This is the picture. Thank God for it. Have we been defeated? Do not let us stay there. "Abram went up out of Egypt,"[2] and he went to "the place where his tent had been at the beginning". Where is the place of our beginning? The House of God made ready for our sinful souls — the Cross. Thank God we have not to travel from Egypt to Palestine, "for to Him who is everywhere, men come not by travelling, but by loving."*

After spiritual defeat, the altar; after spiritual victory, the altar again.[3] I wonder if Satan is ever nearer to us than just when we have "scored a heavy victory"[4] against him. Perhaps he feels anxious then lest we should escape him altogether, and so he clings the closer. As in the Song of Songs (as I read it) a fall caused by spiritual selfishness is followed by the victory of selflessness,[5] so it is here. Abram wins where before he fell. And then (and this is a golden thing) he goes straight to his altar at Mamre — the name means Firmness, Vigour — in Hebron, one of whose two meanings is a Company. "All things through Christ which strengtheneth me" — all firmness, all vigour required for continuance: "Ye are come unto . . . an innumerable company of angels, . . . and to the spirits of just men

*St. Augustine.

made perfect, and to Jesus the Mediator of the new covenant, and to the blood of sprinkling . . . ."[6]

Agag will thrust up his head. He is not hewn to pieces in a day, nor in a month, nor in a year. But we have an altar. By God's grace there will be that hewing of him in pieces that leads to victories like this one of Abram's. Then again, we have an altar, and there we shall find our own Company and the Lord, our Beloved, our Redeemer.

[1]Gen. 13.3, 4.　　[2]v. 1.　　[3]vv. 5-18.　　[4]Rom. 8.37, Souter.
　　[5]S. of S. 5.2 — 6.10.　　[6]Heb. 12.22-24.

2 Cor. 4.10: *Always bearing about in the body the dying of the Lord Jesus, that the life also of Jesus might be made manifest in our body.*

Let the past be. "The past is under the Blood." What of today? Today is ours, and the choice is ours as to how it is to be lived. This verse shows John 15.1, 2 under another figure. There is "dying" in the vine when it is cut back to the bare stalks — a dying to what is the natural desire of the plant. And so if we bear about the dying of our Lord Jesus, it must mean death to much that we naturally desire; but if only we yield our whole being to this "dying", then He is free to manifest His life in any way He chooses, and that is all that matters.

Yesterday someone sent me a passion-flower unlike any I had ever seen before. The stigma was in the form of a cross which extended across the flower in such a way that *everything in the heart of the flower lay under the sign of the cross.* I have never before seen so clearly symbolized the truth that this lovely flower has shown to us.

The Cross: we know what the word connoted when it was spoken by our Lord; and we know that we may not change His thought and speak of the ordinary trouble of life which comes to all, about which there is no choice, in which is no shame or pain, as though such a thing were a cross.   Such trouble would have been ours even had we never known Him.   That kind of trial, though it may be the work of the enemy, turns to fire for purification of the gold; it is part of the discipline of life.   The Cross means shame for His sake, misunderstanding, a pain that would never be but for love of Him, a loss for His Name's sake — loss of a natural, right and lovely joy perhaps — in such things we find the Cross.   There are not many, whose hearts are set on following the Lord, who have not tasted of this cup.

But I know, too, that there are some who almost wonder if their Lord has passed them over; nothing has ever come to them that they could think of as a cross.   They have lived under blue skies from their cradles.   To such I have a word.   It is this: Fear not; no lover of our Lord will be overlooked.   He knows where to find His willing hearts. He will not refuse to His dearest the joy that is bathed in the dews of Gethsemane.

Then let them wait in faith and expectation, only being careful to be ready the moment the Cross is shown.   It may be shown by some inward touch on the spirit.   At that moment let this thought be near: The Hand that touches is the Hand that was pierced — a pierced hand is tender; it knows the feeling of pain.   Or, it may appear in a sudden call from without.   Only let it be recognized and welcomed — I would even write (God enabling our human weakness) *hailed* — with a glorious joy.   The angels must look with longing on those to whom "it is given . . . not only to believe on Him, but also to suffer for His sake";[1] for love longs to suffer for its Beloved. And let us remember the word of the passion-flower; to accept means to accept all that is involved in that acceptance. There are difficult details in the daily crucifixion. If these are debated, there can be no peace. Let the Sign cover everything that is in the heart of the flower, and then, in the silence, "He shall . . . renew thee with His love".[2]

> Lord crucified, O mark Thy holy Cross
> On motive, preference, all fond desires;
> On that which self in any form inspires
> Set Thou that Sign of loss.
>
> And when the touch of death is here and there
> Laid on a thing most precious in our eyes,
> Let us not wonder, let us recognize
> The answer to this prayer.

[1]Phil. 1.29.   [2]Zeph. 3.17, LXX mar.

CHAPTER 13

THE LIFE OF THE WORLD TO COME

EVERY child asks, "What will Heaven be like?" Every grown-up child seeks among the glories and beauties of the earth — sunrise skies, sunsets, all sinless loveliness, music that carries the soul to His feet — for something approaching an answer, till it at last settles down on *Eye hath not seen, nor ear heard . . . .*[1]

But certain words grow to mean Heaven to us. These are my Heaven-words: "We shall be like Him; for we shall see Him as He is."[2] "And His servants shall serve Him: and they shall see His face; and His name shall be in their foreheads."[3]

All the other luminous words scattered through Prophets, Psalms, the Gospels, the Epistles and Revelation, gather round these words and shine on them till they become as "pure gold, like unto clear glass", and we, looking through, see into Heaven.

And till then? — I do not understand the book of Revelation as I wish I did, but chapter 12 shows the triumph of Righteousness, "Therefore rejoice, ye heavens";[4] chapter 13 shows the triumph of unrighteousness, and the word that sums things up is this: "Here is the patience and the faith of the saints."[5] "Here is an opportunity for endurance, and for the exercise of faith, on the part of God's people."[6] Our Lord has conquered sin and pain and death. "Rejoice, ye heavens," and let us rejoice, too, for nothing can shake that glorious fact. And the day is racing towards us when we shall see Him and be like Him.

Till that day comes, "here is an opportunity for endurance, and for the exercise of faith". May the Lord strengthen us all to buy up that opportunity — every minute of it.

[1] Cor. 2.9.   [2] John 3.2.   [3] Rev. 22.3, 4.
[4] Rev. 12.12.   [5] Rev. 13.10.   [6] Weym.

There is one puzzle which comes to all thinking people when a little child is taken to be with the Lord. Did God not give that little one to his parents? We do not go back on our gifts to each other. Does God? Milton got out of the difficulty by thinking of the little one as lent, "Render Him with patience what He lent", but that is not the Bible way. Hannah puts it quite differently. She did not say she would give her loan to the Lord. She said she would lend her gift.[1] And the Spirit of God caused it twice to be recorded that the gifts of God are real gifts (which loans are not). "The gifts . . . of God are without repentance"[2] ("God never goes back on His gifts" is one translation of that). "Every good gift and every perfect gift is from above, and cometh down from the Father of lights, with whom is no variableness, neither shadow of turning"[3] — no variableness, no alteration. He does not change His mind about His gifts to His children, but sometimes He asks for the loan of one of these precious gifts. He does not tell us why He asks for it. He trusts us to trust His love — the love we know so well — and we do trust, and we lend our little treasure, "not grudgingly, or of necessity",[4] but for love's sake, willingly. And we know that He will return what we lent Him when we see Him in the Morning.

[1] Sam. 1.28.   [2] Rom. 11.29.   [3] Jas. 1.17.   [4] 2 Cor. 9.7.

Shall we know one another in Heaven?   Shall we love
and remember?   I do not think anyone need wonder about
this or doubt for a single moment.   We are never told we
shall, because, I expect, it was not necessary to say anything
about this which our own hearts tell us.   We do not need
words.   For if we think for a minute, we know.   Would you
be yourself if you did not love and remember?   David said
that he would go to his baby boy.[1]   What use would there
be in his going to him if he did not know him and love him?
Even people unseen before were recognized by those who
saw them when they came back to earth for a few minutes.[2]
We shall be "as the angels",[3] our Lord said.   Have you ever
noticed how lovingly the angels know and remember?   The
shortest of all the Gospels makes room to tell us (in two
words) how an angel remembered all about a sorrowful
man and thought tenderly of him,[4] knowing, of course, how
sorry he was.   Above all, we are told that we shall be like
our Lord Jesus.[5]   Surely this does not mean in holiness
only, but in everything; and does not He know and love
and remember?   He would not be Himself if He did not,
and we should not be ourselves if we did not.

The wise old *Pilgrim's Progress* has something about this:
Valiant-for-truth says, "Some make a question whether we
shall know one another when we are there."   To this
Greatheart replies, "Do you think they shall know themselves then, or that they shall rejoice to see themselves in
that bliss? and if they think they shall know and do these,
why not know others, and rejoice in their welfare also?"
And Secret, speaking to Christiana says, "They will all be
glad when they hear the sound of thy feet step over thy
Father's threshold."   We know that our loved ones who
have gone before will be glad when they hear the sound
of our feet on the threshold; and we know that we shall all

be glad together when we gather in our Father's House, where "there shall be no more death, neither sorrow, nor crying, neither shall there be any more pain: for the former things are passed away."[6]

[1]2 Sam. 12.23.   [2]Luke 9.30.   [3]Mark 12.25.
[4]Mark 16.7.   [5]1 John 3.2.   [6]Rev. 21.4.

When we are tempted by longings to have with us again those who have passed on, let us think of their eternal joy — "pleasures for evermore."[1] So all the pain is on our side, all the joy is on theirs. It helps to remember this. They will never be rent by longings; they will never be bound by illness; all their bonds are loosed. The more we love them, the more we shall rejoice in their joy. "If ye loved Me, ye would rejoice, because I said, I go unto the Father".[2] That does not mean that there is no sorrow. "Ye shall be sorrowful," our Lord Jesus said — He knew that well — but He went on to say, "your sorrow shall be turned into joy."[3] And ours will be too. Sorrow is not eternal. Joy is eternal. "Weeping may endure for a night [stay with us as a passing guest for a night], but joy cometh in the morning",[4] and stays with us through the day — the long, long day of Eternity.

[1]Psa. 16.11.   [2]John 14.28.   [3]John 16.20.   [4]Psa. 30.5.

Psa. 16.11: *Thou wilt shew me the path of life: in Thy presence is fulness of joy; at Thy right hand there are pleasures for evermore.*

Earthly words can only feel after the beauty of this verse, they cannot quite touch it. One lovely rendering is, "Thou wilt reveal to me the path to life, to the full joy of Thy presence, to the bliss of being close to Thee for ever."

"Close to Thee for ever" — that is Heaven.

Heb. 2.9: *We see Jesus.*

To me, with these words always comes the prayer, *We would see Jesus*[1] (for we are only half beginning to see); and then follows the joy that is the very crown of joy, "We shall be like Him; for *we shall see Him* as He is."[2]

Is it not true that, as we go on day by day saying inwardly, "We would see Jesus", we feel more and more how very little we have seen Him yet? And when we do see Him, we shall feel that we never saw Him at all before — so wonderful, so past imagination, will the greatness of His beauty be. But not only that — and may the joy of these words enfold us — "we shall be like Him; for we shall see Him as He is."

[1]John 12.21.   [2]1 John 3.2.

CHAPTER 14

FRAGMENTS THAT REMAIN

Friendship

IN reading 1 Samuel this morning I noticed afresh certain marks of true friendship:

(1)   The Lord must be between the friends. It must not be A, B, and the Lord; but A, the Lord, and B; "forasmuch as we have sworn both of us in the name of the Lord, saying, The Lord be between me and thee . . . for ever."[1]

(2)   "The soul of Jonathan was knit with the soul of David, and Jonathan loved him as his own soul."[2] But they had to separate, and we hear Jonathan say to David, "Go in peace".

(3)   Later a hard hour had to be faced, but there was no weakening word or softening influence. "Jonathan . . . went to David into the wood, and strengthened his hand in God."[3]

So you can easily test your friendship with anyone by these tests: Who comes first, your Lord or your friend? What is the result of your friendship, strength or weakness?

A friendship which puts the presence of the friend first, and thinks first of the wishes of the friend, and last (if at all) of the will of the Lord, is a curse, and is sure to end in disaster, for it is weakening, hindering and soiling. But a friendship which puts the ungrieved presence of the Lord far first, and thinks always first of His will and His work, is blessed from the first day to the last — only there will never be a last, for the most joyful, wonderful thing about a friend whose golden link is the Lord Himself is that it is timeless. (Did you ever think of how David and Jonathan must be enjoying and loving one another now?) Such a friendship reaches on into what we call Eternity (forgetting that we are in Eternity now); it reaches into the Land of far distances, where there is no more need to say, "Go in peace", for they "shall go no more out."[4]

A selfish friendship is only for today; a selfless friendship is for ever. The golden link of the love of the Lord binds the hearts of such friends together and hallows their friendship. That kind of friendship strengthens, inspires and ennobles.

[1] Sam. 20.42.   [2] Ch. 18.1.   [3] Ch. 23.16.   [4] Rev. 3.12.

* * *

I have noticed that those who can most quickly help a difficult child are those who habitually think kindly — even sometimes, as some would say, too kindly — of others. And I have noticed, too, that it is very hard to pray as one longs to pray for a soul — a sinful, ungrateful, coldly unloving soul — unless one can think of the good that is there, or was there, as well as the evil that is so terribly trying to patience and faith.

There are some things it is well to beware of:

    (1)   Belittling talk of the one who is wrong;
    (2)   Unnecessary talk of the wrong done;
    (3)   Casual judgment;
    (4)   Resentment.

This last is very important. It is extraordinarily easy to slip into what is really personal resentment — a fatal attitude, and one which kills prayer and cuts away any power that might otherwise be ours to help the wrong-doer. "Be deeply moved, but do not sin" is Rotherham's translation of Psalm 4.4, and it is in point here. The Lord keep us under the power of the cleansing Blood when we have to pray for wrong-doers or deal with them.

I have sometimes wondered why the words "Take heed that ye despise not [literally, Take heed that you do not think down upon] one of these little ones" are followed by the parable of the sheep that went astray;[1] and I have wondered whether the reason was something like this:

It is not difficult to be patient with tiresome little lambs. We never think of them in the "thinking down" way that makes it quite impossible to help them. But lambs grow up into sheep, and then it is different. The perverse sheep can try our patience and love very much. Before we know it, we may slip into "thinking down" upon such a one.

There is another danger lying close to all such experiences: it is to lose heart and hope. Perhaps we have toiled long and seem to have effected nothing. The straying sheep seems to care nothing for the fold or even for the Shepherd. So, immediately after the story, we have the words that must have heartened countless thousands of undershepherds: "It is not the will of your Father which is in Heaven, that one of these little ones should perish." Even a grown-up soul is only a "little one" to the Father.

"Now the God of hope fill you with all joy and peace in believing, that ye may abound in hope, through the power of the Holy Ghost."[2]

[1]Matt. 18.10-14. [2]Rom. 15.13.

*   *   *

In a Harmony of the Gospels that I have been given, I found a note about the difference in our Lord's directions to His disciples as they went out to preach. Matthew and Luke say that they were not to take (among other unrequired things) either a staff or sandals, whereas Mark says they were told to take both. The note suggests that Mark told what had been said to Peter (it is believed that he learned much from Peter), and probably Peter and his companion were being sent to a more rugged part of the country where they would each need a good strong stick and a pair of sandals. Does it not show how our Lord knows all about the conditions of our service, and sees to it that we have what we need?

What is your need today? strength? peace? courage? wisdom? He knows all about it. *My God shall supply all your need according to His riches in glory by Christ Jesus.* Phil. 4.19.

*   *   *

Often we wonder how the Lord can possibly go on loving us. Often we are tempted to think that though He may love others, we are different. Do you know what it is to feel so? We are not the first to feel like that. In George Herbert's poem *Assurance* he writes about it; and in another poem, *Gratefulness,* he says,

> "But Thou didst reckon, when at first
>   Thy word our hearts and minds did crave,
>   What it would come to at the worst
>   To save.
>   Perpetual knockings at Thy door,
>   Tears sullying Thy transparent rooms."

Those words were written about 300 years ago. There is unshakable comfort to be found in remembering that our Lord Jesus knew us and all we would be and do *before* He called us. Oh, rest your hearts, you who are troubled, as I rest mine, upon the eternal love of your Lord. *He loveth unto the end.*

Here is just a little song on the never-to-be-enough-wondered-at-love of our dear Lord. ("Thou shalt be called My Pleasure" is from Isaiah 62.4, LXX):

"Thou shalt be called My Pleasure"; who hath dreamed
Of such a name for desert-land redeemed?

And His desire is toward me; O my Lord,
This is indeed a Heavenly wonder-word.

What hast Thou found to be desired in me
In whom is nothing, nor could ever be?

Like sap of life, that, flowing through the bough,
Doth nourish leaf and bud and flower, art Thou.

And as the tree desireth life, so I
Desire my Lord of Life, exceedingly.

But that the Sap should so desire the tree
Is, O Beloved, a wonder unto me.

*   *   *

As I was reading in Genesis 35, I found a very small but very speaking word in the Revised Version of verse 7: "God was *revealed* unto him" — the God who was there all the time was *revealed*.

In the beautiful Beth-el story of chapter 28, there is a Revised Version marginal reading which is full of joy and comfort for us all. There was the ladder and the angels ascending and descending on it; but the Lord Himself stood, not above it but, according to this reading, "beside him", beside poor, weak, wandering Jacob. "Lo, I am with you all the days, and all day long."[1]

Let no one be perplexed by the two readings. Both are true. The Lord our God stands above the ladder; He is eternally above. But — and let us give thanks for that "but" — He is always beside us too.

A very noble Jew, C. O. Montefiore, thought of God as being "near with every kind of nearness". This is a lovely Jewish phrase. God is "near with every kind of nearness" to our beloved ones, "near with every kind of nearness" to us who need Him so sorely today.

The Lord stood beside him. He stands beside you, beside me, with every kind of nearness, and one day the veil will suddenly be drawn back, and "we shall see Him" who has been beside us, with us, all the time, "as He is."[2]

[1]Matt. 28.20, Moule.   [2]1 John 3.2.

*   *   *

In Cumberland, where I used to live, the fields are often bordered by walls of rough grey stones. There is a word in Isaiah that makes me think of those walls: "I will make . . . all thy borders of pleasant stones"[1] ("stones of delight" is Rotherham's lovely rendering).

It is a picture-phrase, a kind of parable. What if the borders (limitations) of our lives, which look so ordinary and often very unbeautiful to us, appear to the eyes of the Spiritual Watchers as full of pleasant stones, stones of delight, jewels of Heaven? Perhaps we lose more than we know when we forget this. The Lord keep us from forgetting. We are meant to live in the power of these spiritual truths, that is, to live as those whose borders are peaceful ("He maketh peace in thy borders"[2]) and beautiful, like walls made of "stones of delight."

[1]Isa. 54.12.   [2]Psa. 147.14.

*   *   *

It was written of a writer who died some years ago, "He was asked to endure the sufferings of those who bring to the world something new."

Our Lord Jesus brought "something new" to the world; and as I have thought specially of the suffering from which He did not shrink, I have found myself wondering if we all realize that *we* are called to bring something new, not to the world as a whole, as He did, but to some part of it; and that if we are to do this we must be ready for what it costs.

To break with all worldly customs; to live utterly separate from the spirit of the world, so that we shall not say, "What is the harm of this and that?" but simply shall have lost all relish for what is not of the Father; to live as those who truly lay all on the altar — time, strength, possessions, literally everything we are and have; to live, not nominally but truly, in unity; this will cost us something. *Are we ready for what it will cost?*

*   *   *

Way's rendering of Colossians 2.7 (used as a help towards understanding the thought within the words which
our Authorized Version gives us) is full of delight to me:
*Be like trees fast-rooted . . . feeling His presence about
you.* Feeling the Presence about us, what can we not be
and do? The tree, deep-rooted, standing up into the air,
feels the presence of that which bathes its leaves, and by the
power of the mystery of life turns that which it feels about
it, and receives within its being, into colour and beauty.
Think of each single leaf which helps to make the green of
our beautiful world. As each tree lives not to itself but
to the forest, so each leaf on each tree lives not to its own
tree only, but to the glory of the whole great mountainside.
What a word for us! Each of us is, as it were, only one
leaf in a great forest. More and more may the Lord make
us as green leaves to others, leaves of refreshment and
coolness in heat, leaves of healing "for bruises and sores",[1]
leaves of joy, too, for in His presence is fulness of joy; and
surely if we grow fast-rooted, feeling His presence about us,
it will be so.

[1]Ezek. 47.12, mar.

* * *

Psa. 68.6, P.B.V.: *He is the God that maketh men to be of
    one mind in an house.*

I thought of this yesterday as I read the following in a
book about ants: "In order to live in permanent common-
wealths (such as the ants') an organism must . . . have an
intense feeling of co-operation, forbearance and affection
towards the other members of its community. . . . Such a
community resembles a perfect republic where each works

for the good of the whole, each having their appointed work, labouring constantly for the good of all, and each ready to sacrifice themselves for the good of all."

Can anyone tell me why it is supposed to be impossible, almost absurd, to count on the Creator of ants and of us, to do for us what He has done for them? Take this pure gold, shining afresh for us: "The household of God"[1] — and "the whole family in Heaven and earth".[2] What words of concord, peace, love, and joy!

[1]Eph. 2.19.   [2]Eph. 3.15.

Eph. 2.13, 14: *But now in Christ Jesus ye who sometimes were far off are made nigh by the blood of Christ. For He is our peace, who hath made both one, and hath broken down the middle wall of partition between us.*

I have read of the finding of a part of the wall of partition to which Paul refers — the very wall upon whose pillars words were written in Roman letters and Greek, forbidding a Gentile to pass the wall — the middle wall of partition. The part found was the block of stone on which the words were written in Greek. Our Lord must have read those words. What were the thoughts in His heart as He read them, knowing what it would cost Him to break down that wall? We know in part, for the Psalms and Prophets tell us. But we can never fathom those deep thoughts. There is something in Calvary that passes our understanding, and words about the Precious Blood should never be read or sung except on the knees of our spirit. Do not let us ever become so accustomed to the thought of it, that we forget what it cost to break down that wall and draw us near.

Prov. 8.27, 30: *When He prepared the heavens, I was there
. . . I was daily His delight, rejoicing always before Him.*

"And He [the Delight of God] bearing His cross went
forth into a place called the place of a skull, which is called
in the Hebrew Golgotha: where they crucified Him, and
two other with Him, on either side one, and Jesus in the
midst".[1]   The Delight of God — crucified.   He who was
as the Jewel set in the heart of that pure glory, when the
God of Heaven and earth prepared the sunrise for this earth;
He to be hanged in shame between two thieves, that our
eyes might see His salvation, which He had prepared before
the face of all people; a Light to lighten the Gentiles, and
the Glory of His people Israel:[2] that we, who sat in darkness, might see a great light; that to us who sat in the region
and shadow of death, light might spring up[3] — words fail,
thoughts fail, before such love.   "O come, let us worship
and fall down: and kneel before the Lord our Maker."[4]

[1]John 19.17, 18.   [2]Luke 2.30-32.   [3]Matt. 4.16.
[4]Psa. 95.6, P.B.V.

*   *   *

Zech. 9.17: *How great is His goodness, and how great is
His beauty!*

Just now I have been seeing something of His beauty in
His lovely flowers.   But "how much better the Lord of them
is: for the first Author of beauty hath created them."[1]
In 2 Esdras 10.55 it is written: "Go thy way in, and see
the beauty and greatness of the building, *as much as thine
eyes be able to see*".   The building there was Zion, but the
words often come to me with deeper meaning.   *As much as*

thine eyes be able to see. How much are our eyes able to see of our Lord Jesus? I have watched people looking through a microscope, glancing for a moment, and then moving away; they have seen nothing. Others look for two or three seconds, say, "How beautiful", and move away; they saw more, but not much. It is only as we look and look, that we really see; and the more we know of the thing at which we look, the more we see in it.

"The excellency of the knowledge of Christ Jesus my Lord: for whom I have suffered the loss of all things . . . *that I may know Him*".[2] How much are we willing to lose that we may know, and so be able to see? It is the *I* in us that blinds our eyes. The loss of *I*, that I may know Him, see Him with new clearness in all creation, in souls loving and beautiful — yes, and in another sense, *un*-lovable, *un*-beautiful — the Lord give this, and more and still more, to us all: this is my prayer. I want more and more to see His goodness and His beauty, not vaguely, intermittently, but truly and continually, in His work, in His dear lovers, in His Book, in Himself.

How great is His goodness, and how great is His beauty! These lovely words seem to me to be pure worship. They lead the heart to those perfect words of worship: "Glory be to God on high, and in earth peace, good will towards men. We praise Thee, we bless Thee, we worship Thee, we glorify Thee, we give thanks to Thee for Thy great glory, O Lord God, Heavenly King, God the Father Almighty. . . . Thou only, O Christ, with the Holy Ghost, art most high in the glory of God the Father. Amen."

[1]Wisdom 13.3.   [2]Phil. 3.8, 10.